# WORD-HOARD

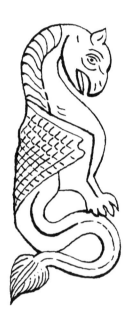

hond ẏſ ʒeſceapod ʒnūme ʒeʒonʒen

# WORD-HOARD

An Introduction to Old English Vocabulary

Stephen A. Barney

with the assistance of

Ellen Wertheimer and David Stevens

New Haven and London    Yale University Press

1977

Copyright © 1977 by Stephen A. Barney.
All rights reserved. This book may not be
reproduced, in whole or in part, in any form
(except by reviewers for the public press),
without written permission from the publishers.

Printed in the United States of America by
The Murray Printing Co., Westford, Mass.

Published in Great Britain, Europe, Africa, and
Asia (except Japan) by Yale University Press,
Ltd., London. Distributed in Latin America by
Kaiman & Polon, Inc., New York City; in
Australia and New Zealand by Book & Film
Services, Artarmon, N.S.W., Australia; and in
Japan by Harper & Row, Publishers, Tokyo Office.


Library of Congress Cataloging in Publication Data

Barney, Stephen A.
    Word-hoard.

    Includes indexes.
    1. Anglo-Saxon language—Glossaries,
vocabularies, etc. I. Title.
PE274.B3      429'.3      76-47003
ISBN  0-300-02026-0

# CONTENTS

INTRODUCTION

This Word-Hoard aims to help a beginning student to
master the more ordinary vocabulary of Old English.  The
total vocabulary of Old English poetry, as preserved in the
six volumes of the Anglo-Saxon Poetic Records, is something
over eight thousand words, of which about sixty percent are
compound words.  But a student need learn only a quarter of
this number of words to know the meanings of over ninety
percent of the running words he will meet in reading Beowulf.  This list is composed of about two thousand words--
those which are most frequent in the poetry a student will
read as he begins to learn OE language and literature.

But the first glance at a page of OE shows that even
learning two thousand words is not the feat of memory which
it may seem.  Of course most of the words are compounds
whose meanings are usually determinable from the meanings
of the bases of which they are composed.  Furthermore, many
of the words are related to each other, and it is obvious
that any systematic attempt to learn vocabulary will advance
much more rapidly by associating related words.  In this
list I have gone farther than the obvious, and have grouped
together all of the words which are etymologically related--
even a number which are not very obvious--in order to assist
the memory.  Once it is known that æðele means "noble," it
is not very hard to learn that æðeling means "nobleman,"
and it is still not very hard to see that ēðel "native land"
is related, and shares in a sense of concern with ancestors,
of genealogical pride.  These connections ease the burden
of learning "Old Anguish," and they can refine the student's
sense of the connotations of words.

vii

In this list I have gathered the 2000-odd words into 227 groups of related words, and arranged these groups in descending order of frequency of all the words in each group. The number to the left of each group is the total count of the appearances of the words of that group in the poems on which I have based this list. The learning of vocabulary, then, will focus on key words, those listed in the "Key-Word Index to the Groups." An early, particularly valuable exercise would be to learn these key words. (The Anglo-Saxons, too, had something like a list of key words: the names of the characters in the runic alphabet [the fuþorc]. Those which are not of doubtful meaning are: feoh "cattle," ūr "aurochs," þorn "thorn," rād "journey," g̊yfu "gift," wynn "joy," hæg̊l "hail," nȳd "need," īs "ice," g̊ēr "year," ēoh "yew," sigel "sun," beorc "birch," eh "horse," mann "man," lagu "water," Ing (the god), ēðel "homeland," dæg̊ "day," āc "oak," æsc "ash," ȳr "yew bow," gār "spear," stān "stone.")

Another aid to the memory is the fact that many of the OE words have relatives in other languages. Because the most helpful language is Modern English, I have been careful to include modern reflexes of OE words. "Modern" here means "after 1500 A.D." Many of these Modern words are no longer used, except perhaps in remote dialects ("taw, dree, wain, bairn, to worth"); nevertheless, most of the Modern reflexes are still vaguely familiar, they are interesting, and they can jog the memory. The "Key-Word Index to the Groups" shows how very few of the groups have no Modern reflex.

Among other related languages I have often given the cognates of OE words which appear in Modern German, Latin, and Greek. The German words are of course closest, and students who know some German will have the easiest time learning OE. The cognates in Latin and Greek are much more obscure, and the connections between these words are often less certain, in spite of the researches that have been undertaken since Jacob Grimm in the early nineteenth century formulated the pattern of relationships between the Germanic and the classical languages. From the Latin cognates can come many mnemonic aids: for example, the English word conceal derives ultimately from the Latin celāre "to conceal." (If you know a Romance language you can often use the Latin cognate even without Latin or without a pair as easy as celāre/conceal.) The OE cognate of

celāre is helan "to conceal" (see No. 82).  The student
will have to see that a Latin c often appears in English
as an h, if he wants to use this mnemonic aid, but he
might prefer remembering in this systematic (and fun) way
to remembering by rote.  And in this case he has another
aid:  HELMet (which conceals the head) is related to
helan.

    The texts on which I have based this list are those
most likely to be read by a student first encountering
OE poetry.  I have used two splendid editions, whose glos-
saries are also word-indexes of all the words which occur
in the texts (although neither editor acknowledges the
fact):  John C. Pope, Seven Old English Poems (Indianapolis
and New York, 1966) and Friedrich Klaeber, Beowulf (Boston,
3rd ed. with 2 supps., 1950).  The former contains the
poems "Cædmon's Hymn," "The Battle of Brunanburh," "The
Dream of the Rood," "The Battle of Maldon," "The Wanderer,"
"The Seafarer," and "Deor."  Whether or not a student uses
this particular edition, he will be likely to read most of
these poems early on.  Klaeber's edition also includes
"The Fight at Finnsburg," but I have left this poem out of
the reckoning.  A frequency list based on these texts
should represent fairly accurately the actual frequencies
of words a beginning student will meet.  Of course most of
the words listed here are also common to  OE prose.  The
vocabulary of this Word-Hoard is skewed toward the secular
and martial in comparison with the whole corpus of OE poetry, but the religious texts are usually read later, and the
peculiarly religious words are usually still obvious in
ModE.

    I have omitted from the list the forms of the verb
"to be," the personal pronouns, the demonstrative pronoun/
definite article sē, sēo, þæt, and the words þe, þæt, and,
on, in (and the relatives of on and in), nē, tō, þā.  I
have also not counted a few high-frequency affixes (e.g.,
a-, be-, ġe-, for-, -līc, and -iġ), but have always noted
this omission in the comments on the group where each such
affix would occur.  Compound words, when they are composed
of two bases each included in groups of high enough frequency to be numbered in this list, are counted twice.
The list breaks off arbitrarily at a group frequency of
twenty.

Two further warnings should be made. The definitions given of the OE words are brief notes, and by no means exhaustive: they define the words only as they are used in the poems I have selected, and even then they cannot register the complex nuances of many words. Also, note that the etymological groupings are of two different orders: some obvious, and some obscure and, even when firmly established, nevertheless conjectural. For instance, in No. 150 it is obvious that winnan "to fight" is related to ģe-winn "battle"; but it is not so obvious (the relationship is much more distant) that winnan is related to wynn "joy." These more remote relationships are given partly because they are interesting; they are only given when authorities appear to agree on them. But surely the Anglo-Saxons would have sensed no connection between wynn and winnan; the recovery of the relationship is an affair of modern philology.

How this list is used will depend on the teacher. If the teacher has students memorize vocabulary, he might simply assign groups of words week by week, with omissions if he sees fit. Perhaps the first dozen or so groups could be skipped, because they are complex and include words of such high frequency that a student learns them quickly simply by reading. Then perhaps twenty groups per week, to finish the list in about eleven weeks. Note that the highest frequency groups contain many of the strong and preterite-present verbs--which after all preserved their unusual conjugations in OE (and ModE) because of their high frequency in speech.

Professor Pope's text has "normalized" spelling, to make it easier for beginners with the language. His normalizations, not so extensive as those of Holthausen and Magoun, seem to me to strike the right compromise for beginners between the actual forms contained in the manuscripts (mainly ca. 1000 A.D.) and the "Early West Saxon" dialect of OE reconstructed by grammarians. I have followed Pope's normalizations, except for words and compounds which appear in Beowulf but not in the poems edited by Pope; these I have usually left in the original spelling (using frequency of spellings as a very rough guide when there is a choice) except when it seemed pointlessly unclear not to normalize slightly. The lists of compounds under each group, therefore, contain spellings not seen in

the head-list of basic words.  I have here and elsewhere
forgone rigid consistency for the sake of clarity.

The words in the head-lists are arranged according to
their importance and frequency, and according to the obvious
progressions of sounds (ablaut and umlaut) and the grammatical forms which they present; here again consistency
has not been the rule.  The words are all identified as to
part of speech: nouns by their gender alone, verbs by their
class alone, and the rest explicitly (adj., adv., prep.,
etc.).  Strong, preterite-present, and anomalous verbs, and
weak verbs with unusual preterite forms, show the "principal parts" after the infinitive form.

Strong verbs are identified with Arabic, weak with
Roman numerals.  So [(ǧe-)healdan (ēo, ēo, ea) (7) "HOLD"]
indicates a strong verb healdan which occurs in our texts
both with and without the ǧe- prefix, without change of
meaning, of class 7, whose principal parts are healdan
(infinitive), hēold (1st and 3rd person, singular, preterite), hēoldon (plural, preterite), and healden (or
ǧe-healden) (past participle).  The infinitives of preterite-present verbs are followed by the forms for the first
and third person present singular, the second person present singular, and the preterite singular (all indicative).

Nouns are identified as masculine, feminine, or neu-
ter, and as wk. (weak) if they are not strong.  Weak adjectives are also identified; if an adjective is used as a
noun, it is identified as sb. (substantive).  Many forms
act as more than one part of speech; rather than repeat
the form, I have the format [ǣr (adv., conj., prep.) "before, ERE" (prefix) "ancient, EARly"].  This may be read
out:  the word ǣr is found as adverb, conjunction, and
preposition, with the meaning (in all cases) of "before"
or "ere."  The word is also used as a prefix, when it
means "ancient" or "early" (as ǣr-ǧewinn "ancient strife").
Furthermore, the ModE words "ere" and "early" are derived
from this group.  The words printed all or partly in capital letters, then, are modern reflexes of the OE words in
this list.  Note that the ModE word printed in capital
letters is not necessarily the direct descendent of the
particular OE form in question, but merely a descendent of
its etymological group.

A slash [/] indicates alternate spellings of an OE
word which are important enough for one reason or another
to include.  Parentheses are used to indicate parts of
words which sometimes, but not always, are joined to the
words in our texts.  If a word has a ġe- prefix without
parentheses, then it always has the prefix in our texts
(but not necessarily in the whole corpus of OE).  If a ġe-
prefixed word is consistently distinct in meaning from its
base word (a radical example is ġe-wītan, No. 52) I have
listed it separately.  The numbers to the left of each
group indicate the frequency of that group's words taken
together.  An asterisk [*] means that the following word
does not occur in any written document, but has been reconstructed as a necessary ancestor-form of some word by
grammarians (e.g., PrimG and IE roots).


I have followed the usage of Pope and Bruce Mitchell
(A Guide to Old English, 2nd ed., New York, 1968) in the
diacritical marks.  A small circle over a ċ or ġ means
that the sounds were palatalized, and are to be pronounced
(according to modern convention) as the "ch" of "church"
and the "y" of "year." (The last sentence could have con-
cluded with the word "respectively"; here and elsewhere
I omit it, letting the reader assume that parallel lists
are respectively ordered.)  Since sc and cg are always
pronounced like "sh" and the "j" of "judge" there is no
need to mark them.  (In a few words, not in this list, like
ascian, the sc is pronounced like the "sk" of "asking.")
The symbols [<] and [>] mean that a form was "derived from"
or is directly "reflected in" another form:  [DAY <dæġ]
means "day, which is directly derived from the OE dæġ."  I
have put macrons ("long marks") over long vowels, and over
the first vowel of long diphthongs (unlike Latin, there are
many short diphthongs in OE).  Throughout, I spell the
voiceless th sound (as in "thin") with a thorn (þ), and its
voiced allophone (as in "then") with an eth (ð).


A hyphen [-] before or after a word indicates its use
as a suffix or prefix, or that a grammatical ending has
been omitted for purposes of illustration.  Hyphenated
forms in head-lists indicate bases used only as compounding
elements in our texts; often these forms will not have
part-of-speech notations.

The terms "cognate," "kin to," and "relative to" refer
to etymological relationships, as far as I am aware of the
present state of philology.  I have relied mainly on
Holthausen, Pokorny, and the OED, but doubtless I sometimes
fail to join what ought to be joined, and join what ought
not to be joined.  A cognate word is not necessarily imme-
diately derived from its kins in this list.

In the lists of compounds, a few important ones are
defined briefly when the meaning is not obvious from the
bases.  The forms which are underlined are the most frequent compounds in the particular set of words (between the
semi-colons); I have underlined a compound only when it
occurs more than three times in our texts and is the most
frequent of the set:  so [. . . ; eormen-, feorh-, fīfel-,
frum-, gum-, mon- "mankind," wyrm-cynn;] means that among
the seven compounds in our texts whose second element is
cynn "nation, kind," the most frequent is mon-cynn which
means "mankind."  Note that the base mon- is not spelled in
the normalized form (mann) because this is the compounds
list; also note that the superior frequency of mon-cynn
does not imply that the other compounds in this set have a
frequency lower than four.

On the important matter of word-formation--the combi-
nations of bases with affixes and the formation of com-
pounds--see Randolph Quirk and C.L. Wrenn, An Old English
Grammar (New York, 1958), Ch. IV; Jess B. Bessinger, Jr.,
A Short Dictionary of Anglo-Saxon Poetry . . . (Toronto,
1960), "Preface"; and Mitchell's Guide mentioned above.

The idea for this list came from the 52-page pamphlet
by John F. Madden, C.S.B.,and Francis P. Magoun, Jr., A
Grouped Frequency Word-List of Anglo-Saxon Poetry (3rd pr.,
Cambridge, Mass., 1961).  Works which I have found inval-
uable in preparing this Word-Hoard are The Oxford English
Dictionary; F. Holthausen, Altenglisches etymologisches
Wörterbuch (Heidelberg, 1934, 1963); A. Campbell, Old
English Grammar (Oxford, 1959, 1964); J.B. Bessinger, Jr.,
and Philip H. Smith, Jr., A Concordance to Beowulf (Ithaca,
1969); J.R. Clark Hall, A Concise Anglo-Saxon Dictionary,
4th ed. with supplement by Herbert D. Meritt (Cambridge,
England, 1894, 1962); J. Bosworth and T.N. Toller, An
Anglo-Saxon Dictionary (Oxford, 1882-98) and its Supple-
ment, ed. Toller (1908-21); Julius Pokorny, Indogerman-

isches Etymologisches Wörterbuch, 2 vols. (Bern and
München, 1955-69).

I am very grateful to a number of people who read parts
of this Word-Hoard and made useful suggestions and correc-
tions:  Joe Harris, Antonette Healey, Traugott Lawler, Ted
Leinbaugh, Robert L. Kellogg, John Pope, Rosemarie Potz,
Robert D. Stevick, David Tandy, Heinrich von Staden,
Robert P. Creed, Bruce Mitchell, and Howell D. Chickering.
Let it not be assumed that they approve of everything here,
or that they share the blame for my errors.

New Haven                                      S.A.B.
March, 1976

# ABBREVIATIONS

| | | | |
|---|---|---|---|
| acc. | accusative | ModG | Modern German |
| adj. | adjective | n. | neuter |
| adv. | adverb | No. | number, refers to a group frequency |
| anom. | anomalous | | |
| cf. | compare | nom. | nominative |
| comp. | comparative | OE | Old English |
| conj. | conjunction | OED | Oxford English Dictionary |
| cpd(s). | compound(s) | | |
| dat. | dative | "our texts" | the poems in Pope's OE Poems and Beowulf |
| dem. | demonstrative | | |
| e.g. | for example | | |
| esp. | especially | pl. | plural |
| etym. | etymology, etymologically | ppl. | past participle |
| | | prep. | preposition |
| f. | feminine | pres. | present |
| gen. | genitive | pret. | preterite |
| Gk. | Greek | PrimG | Primitive Germanic |
| IE | Indo-European | pron. | pronoun |
| ind. | indicative | rel. | relative |
| indef. | indefinite | sb. | substantive |
| interj. | interjection | Scand. | Scandinavian |
| lang(s). | language(s) | sg. | singular |
| Lat. | Latin | Skt. | Sanskrit |
| LWS | Late West Saxon | st. | strong |
| m. | masculine | superl. | superlative |
| MidE | Middle English | vb. | verb |
| ModE | Modern English | wk. | weak |

399

    þǣr (adv.) "THERE" (conj.) "where, if"; þonne (adv.)
"THEN" (conj.) "when" (after comp.) "THAN"; þanan (adv.)
"THENCE"; þēs, þēos, þis (m.,f.,n.) (dem. adj., pron.)
"THIS"; þider (adv.) "THITHER"; þus (adv.) "THUS"; þys-līč
(adj.) "such"; þenden (conj.) "while" (adv.) "meanwhile."

These forms parallel the hw- forms of hwā, etc. (No. 201).
The highly frequent þæt, þē, þā are not counted on this
list: they would fall here. The initial þ- of this group
was unvoiced in OE, but (later spelled th) became voiced by
the time of ModE. The reflexes from this group with voiced
th- are rare sounds in initial position in ModE. Phonolog-
ists have used the pair this'll/thistle to demonstrate the
contrast of voiced and unvoiced initial th-. The cognates
of this "demonstrative group" are omnipresent in the IE
langs.: ModG da, der, dann, denn, dieser "there, the, then,
than, this"; Gk. to "the"; Lat. is-te, tum, tunc, tam "he,
then, then, so," etc. ModE than and then were the same
word in OE, as ModG denn and dann were originally the same.
Cpd.: þǣr-on "therein."


210

    swā (adv.) "SO" (conj.) "as"; swelč/swylč (pron. dem.,
rel.) "SUCH (as)"; swelče/swylče (adv., conj.) "also, as."

Cognate with ModG so, probably Gk. hōs, "as." The OED has
fifteen columns of discrimination of the meaning of "so."
Swelč (Gothic swaleiks) is derived from elements meaning
"so-formed" (swā-līč; cf. hwelč from hwā-līč). The ModE
SUCH derives from the rounded form swylč (a y in OE is
often spelled u in MidE and ModE); the unrounded swelč
gives us dialect variants still heard, even in U.S.A.:
"sech, sich."


201

    hwā, hwæt (pron. interrog., rel.) "WHO, WHAT" (indef.)
"someone, something"; hwæt! (interj.) "listen!"; for-hwon

1

(adv., conj.) "WHY"; hwylč (pron. interrog.) "WHICH" (indef.) "any(one)"; nāt-hwilč (pron. adj., sb.) "someone";
hū (adv., conj.) "HOW"; hwǣr (adv., conj.) "WHERE"; hwonne
(adv., conj.) "WHEN"; hwanan (adv.) "WHENCE"; hwæðer (pron.,
adj.) "which of two, WHETHER"; hwæðer(e) (conj., adv.)
"WHETHER, however, nevertheless"; hwider (adv., conj.)
"WHITHER"; ǣg̊ðer (pron.) "EITHER"; ǣg̊-hwylč (pron.) "each
one"; ǣg̊-hwā (pron.) "every one"; ǣg̊-hwǣr (adv.) "everywhere"; g̊e-hwā (pron.) "each"; g̊e-hwæðer (adj.) "either";
g̊e-hwylč (pron.) "each"; g̊e-hwǣr (adv.) "everywhere."

The compounds of the hwā group with g̊e- and ǣg̊- (see ēče
No. 97) form indefinite pronouns, adverbs, and conjunctions.
It will be seen that the questions a journalist is told to
answer in his first paragraph are all cognate words.  The
suffix -an of hwanan is the usual one to indicate "place
from which" (cf. foran No. 141, ufan No. 151, norðan).
Hwylč (often hwelč) was formed on roots which correspond
to hwā + līč (see No. 30), "of what shape."  The instru-
mental of hwæt, hwī, gives us WHY, not found in our texts
but good OE.  From ǣg̊-hwæðer comes ǣg̊ðer, orig. ā + g̊e-
hwæðer.  This group, parallel to the demonstrative group
(no. 399), may be called the interrogative group.  The IE
etymon of this hw- group may be represented as *kw-,
which appears often as p- in Gk., and as qu- in Lat. (quis,
quid, quo, cum<quum "who, what, how/where, when/accompany-
ing").  The German initial w- yields ModG wer, wie, wenn,
wann, welch, was, wo "who, how, if, when, which, what,
where," etc.
Cpds.:  ō-hwǣr; nō-ðer (=nā hwæðer); wel-hwylč.


197
     of (prep.) "from, OF, out of"; æfter (prep.) "AFTER,
for, in accordance with" (adv.) "AFTERwards"; æftan (adv.)
"from behind"; eft (adv.) "again, afterwards, in turn";
eafora (wk.m.) "son, heir" (pl.) "descendents, retainers."

ModE off was separated from of after the OE period--they
were originally the same word--and new different spellings
and pronunciation distinguished them as adv. and prep.  The
word has various and complex meanings as a prefix (of-,
æf-), among them as perfective, disjunctive, and negative
(e.g., æf-þunca "vexation, i.e. bad-thought," cf. "aver-
sion").  Æfter is not "more aft" but "farther off"

(af + ter, not aft + er) in its historical development.
Like for (No. 141), æfter is not used alone as a conjunction
in OE. Æftan derives from a form like Gothic afta "behind,"
superl. of af "off." Cognate are Gk. apo, Lat. ab, ModG
ab "from." An eafora is one who comes after.
Cpds.: æfter-cweðende; eft-cyme, -sīþ.

## 170

magan (mæg, meaht, meahte) (pret.-pres.) "be able, can,
MAY"; meaht/miht (f.) "MIGHT, power"; mihtig (adj.) "MIGHTY";
mægen (n.) "strength, MAIN, military forces."

The sense "may" for magan is the less likely;*mōtan (No. 46)
usually is used for this meaning. The error is common
because of the ModE derivative. The group is cognate with
the Gk. mēchanē "contrivance" (hence our "machine") from
mēchos "means." Main as in mainland and as in "the Spanish
main" are from mægen, presumably from the notion of a powerful expanse, of land or sea. Our verb might is from the
pret. of magan, now used modally more often than temporally,
as a mark of the subjunctive. The verb may not have been
a pret.-pres. originally, but may have taken on the pret.-
pres. forms by analogy with other vbs. The word mægen is
a special favorite in Beowulf.
Cpds.: æl-, fore-mihtig; ofer-mægen; mægen-āgende, -byrþen,
-cræft, -ellen, -fultum, -rǣs, -strengo, -wudu.

## 162

willan (wolde) (anom. vb.) "wish, be willing, WILL";
nyllan "will not"; willa (wk.m.) "desire, delight"; wilnian
(II) "desire, ask for"; wēl (adv.) "WELL, rightly, indeed";
wela (wk.m.) "WEALth"; welig (adj.) "WEALthy."

Cognate are ModG wollen, Wahl, wohl "to wish, choice, well,"
and Lat. volo, nōlo "I wish (not)." The latter is composed
like nyllan of a negative particle joined to the positive
verb (ne + willan = nyllan); cf. nyt, nān, nis, nabban,
etc. from wit, ān, is, habban, etc. From wille iċ, nylle
iċ "whether I wish to, or not" comes willy-nilly. OE (like
all the Germanic langs.) has no formal future tense; in
poetry, futurity is usually signalled by context (with the
present tense form of the verb), and rarely by the ModE
method of willan or sculan (No. 124) + infinitive (usually

with some hint of the desire or obligation implied by the
verbs). In MidE the word wealth was superfluously used
along with the older word WEAL on the analogy of "health."
Willan and wĕl reflect different ablaut grades of an IE
root; the Gothic forms are wiljan and waila.
Cpds.: wēl-hwylċ, -þungen; wil-cuma, -ġeofa, -ġesīþ, -sīþ;
ǣr-, burh-, eorþ-, hord-, māððum-wela.


159

     eal(l) (adj., sb.) "ALL" (adv.) "entirely"; ealles (gen.
sg. as adv.) "completely"; nealles/nalles (ne + ealles) "not
at all."

The ModE vowel a in ALL derives from the Mercian form alle.
The LWS dialect of our texts shows "breaking" (diphthong-
ization) of the æ, which comes from the Germanic a, to ea
(pronounced æa), so *all >*æll >eall in West Saxon. (It
is assumed that all a's from PrimG were changed to æ in OE
if not followed by m or n.) In the more northerly dialects
(Anglian, which includes Mercian) from which modern Standard English derives, *all >*æll which "retracts" to all
again. The rule is that before h, u(w), l + consonant, and
r + consonant, the vowel æ breaks to ea in West Saxon. The
word has no certain cognates outside the Germanic langs.
From eall + swā come "also," hence "as" (cf. ModG also,
als). The gen. pl. of eall is ealra, Anglian alra, whence
MidE aller-, alder- meaning "of all," and Shakespeare's
alderliefest "dearest of all." The use of the gen. sg. ad-
verbially in ealles is common; cf. our "nights" for "at
night."
Cpds.: eal-fela, -ġearo, -īren; æl-mihtiġ; al-walda (an
Anglian form).


151

   man(n) (dat. sg., nom. pl. men) (m.) "MAN"; man (indef.
pron.) "one."

The i-umlauted vowels of the dat. sg. and nom./acc. pl. re-
veal original case endings which contained an i. Mann
serves for both "adult male" and "human being (of either
sex)," in English; the other Germanic langs. adopted distinct words for the two senses: ModG Mann and Mensch "human
being." The latter form occurs in OE (not in our texts)

as mennisc (adj.) "human(s)," which survived to the 12th
c. The OE terms which discriminate sexes are wer (Lat.
vir) and wīf (+ man = woman). ModG, like OE, has man in
nom. (unstressed) meaning "one" (cf. French on).
Cpds.: man-cynn, -drēam, -dryhten, -þwǣre; brim-, ealdor-,
fyrn-, glæd-, glēo-, gum-, hired-, iū-, lid-, sǣ-, wǣpned-
mann.

151
    ofer (prep.) "OVER, above, across" (prefix) "excessive";
ufan (adv.) "from abOVE"; ufor (comp. adv.) "further up";
ufera (comp. adj.) "later"; up(p) (adv.) "UP(wards)"; uppe
(adv.) "UP"; yppe (wk.f.) "raised floor, high seat."

Cognates Gk. hyper, Lat. super "above, beyond," ModG über,
ober, oben "over" and auf "upon."
Cpds.: ofer-cuman, -flēon, -flitan, -gān "pass over,"
-helmian, -hīġian, -hycgan, -hyġd, -mæġen, -māððum, -mōd,
-sēcan, -sēon, -sittan, -swimman, -swȳðan, -weorpan; upp-
gang, -lang, -riht, -rodor.

150
    wynn (f.) "joy, delight"; (ġe-)wunian (II) "dwell,
remain (with), inhabit"; wennan (I) "accustom (someone) to,
entertain"; wēn (f.) "expectation, hope"; wēnan (I) "expect,
suppose, WEEN, hope"; wine (m.) "friend, friendly lord";
winnan (a,u,u) (3) "contend, fight"; ġe-winnan (3) "WIN,
achieve"; ġe-winn (n.) "strife, battle"; wīscan (I) "WISH."

The Lat. cognate venus "loveliness, Venus" probably gives
the original sense of the group, which combines love and
war. One takes delight (wynn, ModG Wonne) in a friend
(wine) to whom one is accustomed (wunian), and one has
great expectations for him (wēn), and may strive for him
(winnan). The ModE pair habit/habitation helps account
for the ideas of dwelling (ModG wohnen "to dwell") and custom (ModG gewöhnen "to accustom") joined in the group.
ModG wünschen "to wish" preserves the n, missing from
wīscan. Winnan is connected with the group as are connected the two senses of the Skt. cognate vánati "desired, ob-
tained." What is hope (wēn) in OE has become merely delu-
sion in the ModG cognate Wahn. The word wine is easily
confused with wīn (n.) "WINE" (the beverage).

Cpds.: wynn-lēas, -sum; ēðel-, hord-, līf-, lyft-, symbel-
wynn; be-wennan; or-wēna; frēa-, frēo-, g̊eō-, gold-, gūþ-,
mǣg̊-wine; wine-dryhten, -g̊eōmor, -lēas, -mǣg̊; ūr-, fyrn-,
ȳþ-g̊ewinn.

## GROUPS 11-20

141

for(e) (prep.) "FOR, beFORE, in place of" (as prefix,
intensive, often destructive, perfective); fore (adv.)
"thereFORE"; forþ (adv.) "FORTH, away"; g̊e-forþian (II) "ac-
complish" (perfective of "to further"); furður (adv.) "FUR-
THER"; (g̊e-)fyrðran (I) "FURTHER, impel"; furðum (adv.)
"recently, first"; foran (adv.) "before"; forma (wk. super-
lative adj.) "FIRST"; fyrmest (superl. adj.) "first, FORE-
MOST"; fruma (wk.m.) "beginning, chief."

The same root gives ModG für and vor, Gk. para, peri-, Lat.
prō-, prāe, per- (the last also a "perfective" prefix,
like ModG "ver-"). Ultimately the pr- of Gk. prōto and Lat.
primus "first" is cognate. The use of for alone as a conjunction does not occur in English before the 12th c.; in
OE for + þon, þȳ, þǣm, hwon, hwȳ (compounded or not) served
as "therfore, because, wherefore, why" etc. Note that the
OE fyrst (frist) "a space of time" (ModG Frist) is not a
member of this group and does not mean "first." ModE
FIRST is derived from a homophone fyr(e)st (ModG Fürst
"prince") which would fall here but does not occur in our
texts. Like g̊e-, for- as a prefix sometimes gives a verb
a perfective mood, indicating the completion of the action
of a verb (for-bærnan means "to burn up completely"). It
also is frequent as a first element in adverbial and con-
junctive compounds (e.g., for-þon). For- and fore- as compounding elements or prefixes are not counted here.
Cpds.: æt-, be-foran; dǣd-, hild-, land-, lēod-, ord-,
wīg̊-fruma; frum-cynn, -gār, -sceaft "creation"; forþ-
g̊eorn, -g̊erīmed, -g̊esceaft, -g̊ewiten, -weg̊.

140

beran (æ, ǣ, o) (4) "BEAR, bring, wear"; -berend
"bearing, having"; -byrd (f.) "BURDEN, responsibility";
g̊e-bǣran (I) "behave"; bǣr (f.) "BIER"; byrele (m.) "cup-

bearer"; ǧe-boren (ppl. adj.) "BORN, born together, broth-
er"; bearn (n.) "child, BAIRN, son"; byre (m.) (1) "son,
boy" (2) "opportunity"; ǧe-byrdo (wk.f.) "child"; -bora
(wk.m.) "bearer"; bearm (m.) "bosom, lap."

Related to Gk. pherō, Lat. fero "I carry."  Presumably one's
bearm is where one carries things; a ship's bearm is its
hold.  One's bearing is still an index of one's behavior.
ModE BIRTH is a reflex of byrd in a sense not represented
in our texts.  Bearn is easily confused with beorn (m.)
"warrior."
Cpds.: æt- "bear away," for-, on-, oþ-beran; helm-, sāwl-,
reord-, gār-berend; dryht-bearn; mund-byrd; bearn-ǧebyrdo;
wǣǧ-bora.


131
    eald (adj.) "OLD"; ieldra (comp.) "older"; ieldesta
(superl.) "oldest"; ealdian (II) "grow old"; ieldu (f.)
"old age"; ieldu (m.pl.) "men (of old)"; ieldan (I) "delay";
ealdor (m.) "chief, prince, ALDERman"; ealdor (n.) "life."

The idea that an older man becomes a chief (ealdor) is obvious; for the idea that oldness and "life" (ealdor) are
connected, compare the words "age" and "aged," and the word
weorold (No. 47).  Cognate are ModG alt, Alter "old, age"
and Lat. alere "to nourish" (>alma mater "foster mother");
hence the idea of eald is from an idea of growing up (Gothic
and OE alan "to nourish, grow").
Cpds.: eald-fæder, -ǧeseǧen, -ǧesīþ, ǧestrēon, -ǧewinna,
-ǧewyrht, -hlāford, -metod, -sweord; ealdor "chief" -lēas,
-mann, -þeǧn; ealdor "life" -bealu, -cearu, -dagas, -ǧedāl,
-ǧewinna, -lang, -lēas.


129
    gōd (adj., sb.n.) "GOOD"; bet- (adv.) "better"; betera
(comp. wk. adj.) "BETTER"; betst (superl. adj.) "BEST";
bōt (f.) "remedy, reparation"; ǧe-bētan (I) "improve, remedy"; sēl (comp. adv.) "better"; sēlra/sēlla (comp. wk.
adj.) "better"; sēlest (superl. adj.) "best"; sǣl (m.,f.)
"time, occasion, happy time"; ǧe-sǣliǧ (adj.) "prosperous,
happy"; ǧe-sǣlan (I) "befall, turn out favorably."

The "gather" group (No. 31) may be related to gōd; if so,
the original idea would be "consent, suitability" and hence

goodness. The long vowel distinguishes it from gŏd "God."
The ModG cognate gut also has comp. and superl. forms bes-
ser and best. These latter, and their OE alternates sēlra
and sēlest, are not etym. related to gōd; they are degrees
of other adjectives whose positive degree no longer survived. The OE kins of betera and sēlra, bōt and sǣl (cf.
ModG Busse "penance," selig "blessed, happy") suggest their
original senses of reparation and prosperity. We still use
"better" in the sense of a mere return to a normal state
("It's all better"). The word ge-sǣlig̊ has shown a remarkable history; from the notion of "blessed" still present in
ModG came in English a sense of "innocent," whence "naive,"
whence SILLY. We use the reflex of bōt, BOOT, in the
phrase "to boot" meaning "in addition": "an advantage" was
taken as "something additional thrown in." In Beowulf,
sǣl is twice used with its synonymous rhyme-word mǣl "suit-
able time" in happy formulas: "Þā wæs sǣl ond mǣl" ("then
was a time of joy"--1. 1008); "sē ğeweald hafað / sǣla ond
mǣla" ("he [God] who has control over times and seasons"--
11. 1610-11).
Cpds.: ǣr-gōd "antique and fine"; gōd-fremmend; bet-līc̊;
weorold-ğesǣlig̊.


128
     (ğe-)standan (stōd, stōdon, standen) (6) "STAND, take
a stand"; stede (m.) "place, position"; staðol (m.) "foundation, firm position"; ğe-staðolian (II) "establish, confirm"; stǣlan (= staðolian) (I) "establish, impute, avenge";
stellan (I) "place, establish"; (ğe-)steall (m.,n.) "place,
foundation, site"; ğe-stealla (wk.m.) "companion"; stǣl
(m.) "place, position"; stille (adj.) "steady, STILL"; stōl
(m.) "seat, throne"; stefn (m.) (1) "prow, STEM of a ship"
(2) "trunk of a tree"; stefna (wk.m.) "STEM of a ship";
stefnettan (II) "stand firm"; stōw (f.) "place"; -steald
(n., adj.) "dwelling, situated"; stæþ (n.) "bank, shore."

This complex group, founded on an IE root *sta- and its ablaut variants, is cognate with Lat. stāre, status, sistere
"to stand, status, to place (cause to stand)" and the huge
number of derivatives from these words (e.g., estate, con-
stitute, statute, stay, persist, stable, stanza, establish,
stationery); with Gk. stēnai, stasis, stoa "to stand, stasis, pillared hall" (statics, ecstatic, Stoic); with ModG
stehen, Stand, stellen, Stamm, Stall, Stuhl, Statt, ver-

stehen, Stadt, Gestade "to stand, position, to place, stem, stall, chair, place, to understand, town, shore"; and with words in all the IE langs. except Armenian and Albanian. The reflex of stōl, "STOOL," shows some degeneration of meaning. Stede and stōw are places where one stands (often military); a stæþ is a place to stand when disembarking from a boat. Staðol and its derivatives have an important religious connotation of security and heavenly confirmation. Stefn has apparently unrelated homophones meaning "voice" (f.) and "time, occasion" (m., like stefn "prow"); but the variant of our stefn, stemn "prow" or "stern," reveals its origin as the beam (tree-stem) to which the side boards of a boat were attached, as in the nautical term "from stem to stern." The compounds of ģe-stealla rise from a military sense of one's "taking a stand by another person," being his "companion-in-arms." The present tense (and ppl.) of the base verb has "n-infix" (cf. Lat. vinco, vīci) not found in the preterite, so standan/stōd (cf. wæcnan/wōc "waken") and ModE stand/stood. Cpds.: ā-, æt-, be-, for-, wiþ-standan; bǣl-, burh-, camp-, folc-, hēah-, mæðel-, wīc-, wong-stede; stede-fæst; ā-, on-stellan; weall-steall; eaxl-, fyrd-, hand-, lind-, nȳd-ģestealla; brego-, ēðel-, gum-, ģief-stōl; wæl-stōw "place of slaughter, battlefield"; hæģ-steald; in-ģesteald; bunden-, hringed-, wunden-stefna.


## 127

   mid (prep.) "with, together with, by means of" (adv.) "in attendance, at the same time."

Completely lost from ModE (amid is not cognate in spite of its sense) except possibly in midwife "with the woman" even though mid was the regular word for our "with" (of accompaniment). Cognates: ModG mit, Gk. meta-.


## 124

   ān (adj., pron.) "ONE, lone"; nān "not one, NO"; ān- "single, lone"; ānunga (adv.) "entirely"; ānga (wk. adj.) "sole"; (n)ǣniģ (pron., adj.) "ANY, anyone, not any"; ān-līċ (adj.) "unique, beautiful"; āna (adv.) "alone"; ǣne (adv.) "once."

The o of ModE "one" characteristically appears for a West
Saxon ā of our poetic texts (cf. stān "stone," hwā "who").
The initial w sound of ModE "one," not spelled, developed
around the fifteenth century (still missing from ONLY < ān-
līċ). Etym. related to Lat. ūnus, and curiously to the
words onion, ounce, inch, uncial, eleven, atone. The high
frequency of this group in the elegies suggests their theme;
āna in Beowulf esp. indicates heroic single-handed derring-
do. Nān of course = ne + ān.
Cpds.: ān-feald, -floga, -genga, -haga, -pæþ, -tīd.


124
    sculan (sceal, scealt, scolde) (pret.-pres.) "SHOULD,
ought to, must, SHALL"; scyldiġ (adj.) "guilty."

The ModG cognate is sollen. The future sense "shall" of
sculan, most common in ModE, is rare in our texts; the sense
of obligation is dominant (see No. 162). Scyldiġ is related
through an idea of debt: Gothic skula, ModG Schuld "debt,"
hence "guilt." ModE "shilly-shally" corresponds to shall
I, shall I (not); cf. willy-nilly.


117
    dryhten (m.) "lord, chief"; dryht (f.) "band of re-
tainers, noble company"; dryht- "lordly, splendid"; drēogan
(ēa, u, o) (2) "perform, undergo, endure."

The Gothic ga-drauhts "soldier" is related to the Gothic
driugan "to do military service"; hence the relation of
dryht and its chief the dryhten to drēogan. The idea of
suffering often felt in drēogan may well reflect its early
military sense as in the Gothic (cf. "drudge"). Like many
old martial and royal terms, dryhten provided Christian
authors with a word for God. Drēogan survives in the dialect phrase dree one's weird "endure one's fate" (on
weird see No. 102), but the important OE word dryhten is
lost in ModE.
Cpds.: frēa-, frēo-, gum-, mon- "liege lord," siġe-, wine-
dryhten; enġel-, mago-dryht; sibbe-ġedryht; dryht-bearn,
-guma, -līċ, -līċe, -māðum, -scype, -sele, -sib; ā-drēogan.

116

cyning (m.) "KING"; cyne- "royal"; cynn (n.) "race, family, KINdred, KIND"; ġe-cynde (adj.) "innate, natural"; cennan (I) "beget"; -cund (adj.) "deriving from, KIND."

Cognate with Lat. gens "race, family," genus "kind," (g)nātus "born," ModG Kind "child." Cyning derives either from cynn "nation" + patronymic suffix -ing, or from cyne- "royal" + -ing. Note the homophones cennan (1) "beget" and (2) "make known" (No. 90). The cognate relation of Lat. nātus to English cynn justifies the frequent MidE trans- lation of natura as kinde (hence Shakespeare's "kind" ≈ "natural, familial"). Manna cynn(es) is a frequent formula. Cpds.: beorn-, eorþ-, folc-, gūþ-, hēah-, lēod-, sǣ-, sōþ-, þēod- "king of a people," worold-, wuldor-cyning; cyning- bald, -wuldor; cyne-dōm, -rīċe; eormen-, feorh-, fīfel-, frum-, gum-, mon- "mankind," wyrm-cynn; ā-cennan; feorran- cund.


GROUPS 21-30

114

ǣr (adv., conj., prep.) "before, ERE" (prefix) "an- cient, EARly"; ǣr-þon (conj.) "before"; ǣror (comp. adv.) "before, earlier"; ǣrra (comp. adj.) "former"; ǣrest (superl. adv., adj.) "first, at the earliest."

The word ǣr is itself a comparative form, from *airiz the comp. of *air "early." So ǣror and ǣrra are double com- paratives, the former composed in OE times, the latter in PrimG. ModE EARLY derives from *ar or ǣr + līċe. The adv. ǣr is often used to give pluperfect force to a preterite verb: þæt hē ǣr ġespræc means "what hē had said." Cpds.: ǣr-dæġ, -fæder, -gōd, -ġestrēon, -wela, -ġeweorc, -ġewinn.


108

habban (hæfde) (III) "HAVE, hold"; -hæbbend(e) "equipped with."

Whether the word is cognate with hebban "lift" (>HEAVE) or Lat. habēre (or, more likely, capere "seize") is disputed. Remarkable is the reduction of the verb, esp. in its aux- iliary use, from habban to a as in "He'd 'a seen" (hē wolde habban ġesewen).

Cpds.: for-, wiþ-habban; bord-, lind-, rond-, searo-
hæbbend(e).


102

(ġe-)weorðan (wearþ, wurdon, worden) (3) "become, happen, (aux.) be"; -weard "(to-)WARD"; wyrd (f.) "fate,
WEIRD (personified)"; wierdan (I) "injure, destroy."

The verb survives in ModE in the phrase "wo worth the day!"
meaning "evil befall the day!" The IE root has the idea
"to turn," hence "turn into" > "become." So the Lat. cognates are vertere "to turn" and versus "furrow," or a "line"
of verse, where the ox or pen turns back. The OE auxiliary
use of weorðan occurs as well in ModG werden. The weird
sisters of Macbeth are the "fatal" or "destiny-knowing"
ones; the Icelandic Urðr (cognate with wyrd) is one of the
Norns. The variation of ð and d in the different forms of
weorðan illustrates Verner's Law.


101

gangan (ēo, ēo, a) (7) "go"; ġe-gangan (7) "reach, get,
happen"; gengan (I) "go"; gang (m.) "going, passage, flow";
-genga (wk.m.) "goer"; -genge (adj.) "going"; gān (ēode)
(anom. vb.) "GO"; ġe-gān (anom. vb.) "get, undertake, happen."

Gangan may be a lengthened form of gān, or gān may be a
shortened form of gangan by analogy with standan, with its
shortened alternate form in Germanic, ModG stehen. The ġe-
forms of both verbs are good examples of "perfective" meanings. Cognate are ModG Gang and Gänger "passage, goer."
The preterite of gān is from a separate verb ēode, otherwise lost, which may have been related to the Lat. īre "to
go." The word ēode became yode in MidE, but 16th c. archaizing writers used yede.
Cpds.: ā-gangan; be- "circuit, expanse," in-, upp-gang;
ān-, in-, sǣ-genga; ūþ-genge; full-, ofer- "pass over,"
oþ-, ymb-gān.


101

mōd (n.) "mind, heart, MOOD, high spirit"; mōdiġ (adj.)
"bold, courageous"; ġe-mēde (n.) "consent"; an-mēdla (wk.m.)

"arrogance, pomp."

The ModE derivatives mood, moody miss the powerful sense
of mōd, as do the ModG cognates Mut, Gemüt.  Related to the
(Doric) Gk. mōsthai "covet," perhaps Lat. mos "custom, will."
Gothic mōþs means "anger, emotion."
Cpds.: āwisc-, bolgen-, ēaþ-, g̊alg-, g̊eōmor-, gūþ-, hrēoh-,
ofer-, sārig̊-, glæd-, stīþ-, swīþ-, wērig̊-, yrre-mōd; fela-
mōdig̊; mōdig̊-līc̊e; mōd-cearu, -c̊earig̊, -g̊ehyg̊d, -g̊eþonc,
-g̊iōmor, -lufu, -sefa "mind, spirit," -þracu, -wlanc.


## 99

       (g̊e-)dōn (dyde) (anom. vb.) "DO, perform"; dǣd (f.)
"DEED"; dōm (m.) "judgement, reputation, glory, choice";
dēman (I) "judge, DEEM"; dēmend (m.) "judge, God"; dǣdla
(wk.m.) "doer."

The IE root signifies "to place, set, put"--hence don and
doff (do + on, do + off) refer to the placement of the hat.
A thing established is a judgement, so our dōm (whose modern reflex DOOM has lost its sense of "judgement" in favor
of a sense of the fate which impends, the finality of dooms-
day) is cognate with the Gk. themis "justice personified"
via the IE root *dhē-:*dhō-.  (These conjectured IE forms
show the "ablaut" of vowels in a regular series of gradation
which accounts for the quality of all vowels in IE, and is
most visible to us in the vowel gradations of the stems of
strong verbs.)  A thesis (Gk.) likewise is a thing set down
or proposed; the Lat. cognates have the sense "put":  ab-
dere, condere, dēdere "to put away, put together, give up."
The root may be the source of the dental suffix which forms
the pret. of Germanic weak verbs (cf. our modern DID + infinitive = pret.).  Dōm and dēman exhibit the effects of
i-umlaut.
Cpds.: dǣd-cēne, -fruma, -hata; ellen-, fyren-, lof-dǣd;
dōm-dæg̊, -g̊eorn, -lēas; cyne-, wīs-dōm; mān-for-dǣdla.


## 97

       ēc̊e (adj.) "eternal" (adv.) "eternally"; ā, āwa (adv.)
"always"; nā/nō (adv.) "never, not at all"; æfre (adv.)
"EVER"; næfre (adv.) "NEVER"; ǣg̊- (prefix of indefinite
generalization) "each, every, any."

The frequent word ḗċe (esp. in the formula ḗċe Dryhten) is
not used after the 13th c.  It is formed on the root (as in
Gothic aiw) from which derive ā̆ and ā̆wa (and ModG ewig
"eternal").  Cognate are ModG je "ever," Gk. aiōn, Lat.
aevum "lifetime, aeon."  Less certain is the relation of
ǣfre to this group:  it may represent *ā-in-feore "ever in
life," but this is admittedly doubtful.  The very common
prefix ǣ̊ġ- (see esp. the hwā group No. 201) represents ā̆
"always" + ġe- (indefinite prefix).  The word ġe-hwā means
"each (one)," and ǣ̊ġ-hwā means "every one."  Words with this
prefix are not counted in this group.  A ModE reflex of the
root of ā̆ is "ay(e)," (often in the phrase, for ay), some-
what archaic, which rhymes with "say" and is distinct from
"aye" meaning affirmative as a vote (homophone of "eye").
(Strictly, "ay" is a Norse loan-word, itself derived from
the Germanic root from which ā̆ springs.)  OE sōna "forth-
with" and ġēna "further" contain ā̆ in unstressed form, but
the words are not counted here.


97
    fela (indeclinable pron.) "much (of)" (adv.) "much";
full (adj.) "FULL (of)" (adv.) "wholly, FULLy, very" (n.sb.)
"(filled) cup, beaker" (prefix) "following, serving";
fyllu (wk.f.) "FILL, plenty, feast"; fultum (m.) "help,
support"; fylstan/ful-lǣstan (I) "help"; folgian (II)
(= full-gān, anom. vb.) "FOLLOW, pursue"; folgoþ (m.) "position of service, FOLLOWing, office."

Fela was originally an adjective, from which the adverb
was derived (acc. sg. n.); the adverb took on a substantive
function, often with a genitive, but retains a feature of
adverbs, being "indeclinable," or showing no variation of
ending.  Adverbs are also made from the gen. (ealles) and
dat. (ealle) of adjectives.  The notion of "service" in compounds of full appears to arise from a sense of filling as
satisfying, hence providing satisfactory service (cf. "supplement" from Lat. plēre "to fill").  Ful-lǣstan and ful-
gān (in the form full-ēode) occur in our texts; the forms
fylstan and folgian may not have been recognized as identical: cf. stǣlan/staðolian (No. 128); wer/weorold (No. 47).
Likewise fultum is full + tēam (<tēon) "service-provision":
rarely in OE is it spelled fulteam.  Cognates in ModG are
viel, voll, folgen "much, full, to follow"; Gk. polys "much,"
plērēs "full" (whence pleroma, the "fullness" of Gnostic

and theological terminology); Lat. plēre, plūs "to fill, more."
Cpds.:  eal-fela; fela-fricgende, -ġeōmor, -hrōr, -mōdiġ; eġes-, sorh-, weorþ-ful; medo-, sele-ful (as "beaker"); wæl-, wist-fyllu; mæġen-fultum.

## 96

(ġe-)witan (wāt, wāst, wiste) (pret.-pres.) "know"; nytan "not know"; bewitian (II) "watch"; wita (wk.m.) "wise man"; (ġe-)witt (n.) "intelligence, senses"; wītiġ, ġe-wittiġ (adj.) "wise"; wīs (adj.) "WISE"; wīse (wk.f., and suffix) "manner, way"; ġe-wiss (adj.) "trustworthy, certain"; wīsian (II) "guide, show the way"; wīsa (wk.m.) "leader."

The archaic ModE verbs "to WIT, to WOT" and the ModE noun WIT are obviously derived from this group.  The IE sense of the etymon is "see":  "to have seen" is "to know."  So the cognates in Gk. are eidos "appearance" (>idol) and idea "form"; in Lat. the important cognate is vīdēre "to see," whence come many ModE derivatives.  Witan is related to wītan "blame," and ġe-wītan "go" (No. 52), but the groups are separated in this list simply to avoid undue complexity. The translation of wīsian, "guide," is itself a ModE word borrowed from French, and the French word was borrowed from an early German (Frankish) form of witan.  ModG cognates are wissen, Weise, weisen, Witz, gewiss, Gewissen "to know, manner, to direct, witticism, certain, conscience." Cpds.:  nāt-hwylċ "someone (I know not who)"; ūp-, fyrn-, rūn-wita; fyr-witt; wīs-dōm, -fæst, -hycgende; wis-līċ; ġe-wis-līċe.

## 93

wīġ (n.) "war, combat, martial power"; wīgan (I) "fight"; ġe-wegan (æ, ǣ, e) (5) "fight"; wīġend (m.) "warrior"; wiga (wk.m.) "warrior."

Cognate with Lat. vīci "I conquered."  The word ġe-wegan is distinct from its homophone wegan (5) "carry" (No. 49). As often, a present participle (wīġend) has been made into a noun (cf. friend, fiend--hence the e follows the i).  The group is lost entirely from ModE; the mass of compounds show how easily these words came to the minds of poets in search of the frequent initial w.

Cpds.: wīg̊-bealu, -bill, -bord, -cræft, -cræftig̊, -freca, -fruma, -g̊etawa, -g̊eweorðad, -gryre, -haga, -heafola, -hēap, -heard, -hete, -hryre, -plega, -sigor, -smiþ, -spēd, -weorð-ung; fēðe-wīg̊; gār-wīg̊end; æsc-, byrn-, gār-, gūþ-, lind-, rand-, scyld-wiga.

## GROUPS 31-40

90

    cuman (ō, ō, u) (4) "COME, go"; cuma (wk.m.) "visitor"; cyme (m.) "coming, arrival."

Often forms of cuman appear with w after the c, revealing the connection with the IE root *gwem-. The Lat. venīre "to come," cognate with cuman, shows the survival of the w and the loss of the initial consonant in that branch of the IE group. The o of the ModE spelling derives from the medieval spelling of o for u before groups of "minims" (like the i-shaped strokes in u, m, n) to avoid confusion--the spelling here indicates no sound change (cf. monk for munk, both pronounced the same). Our "become," from "be come," to have arrived, has driven out weorðan "become." The ModE becoming "apt, nice," is from this verb, but ModE "comely" is from a separate root represented in OE cȳme "beautiful." Cpds.: be-, ofer-cuman; cwealm-, wil-cuma; eft-cyme.

90

    cunnan (cann, canst, cūðe) (pret.-pres.) "know, know how, be able, CAN"; cūþ (adj.) "known, familiar, COUTH"; cȳþþ (f.) "known region, home"; (g̊e-)cȳðan (I) "make known, announce"; cunnian (II) "test, find out by experience, try"; cennan (I) "make known"; (g̊e-)cnāwan (ēo, ēo, ā) (7) "KNOW, recognize, perceive"; cēne (adj.) "bold, KEEN"; fracod/forcūþ (adj.) "wicked"; on-cȳþþ (f.) "grief."

The present of cunnan was formed on the preterite of a verb meaning "to learn"; "to have learned" is "to know." Hence the pret.-pres. form; a new pret., signalled by the dental ð, was formed on the old strong preterite. The group is related to Lat. (co)gnōscere "to be acquainted," nōvī "I know" (itself a pret.-pres. verb: to have been acquainted is to know). The ModE pret. of can, could, includes its l by analogy with should and would, which have l historically (scolde, wolde). The loss of the n before the ð of cūðe is

characteristic of OE and its most closely related langs.,
Old Saxon and Old Frisian, in the West Germanic Group.  So
we have tooth instead of *tonth for the ModE cognate of the
Lat. stem dent-, and we have mouth instead of something like
the ModG Mund "mouth."  ModE con "to learn" was distinguished from can "to be able" in the MidE period.  One's
native land is where one's dear ones are, one's KITH (from
cȳþþ) as in "kith and kin."  KEN, CUNNING, CANNY also derive from this group, and the term kenning (from Icelandic).
The relation of cēne to this group is uncertain (PrimG
*konj-).  To be intensely uncouth is to be forcūþ.  The
cunnan group may be related to the cyning group (No. 116);
if so, kith is cognate with kin.  Note cennan "make known"
has the homophone cennan "beget."  Also note the sometimes
confusing forms of the verbs cunnan and cunnian.
Cpds.:  cūþ-līċe; un-cūþ, wīd-cūþ "famous"; ā-cȳðan; dǣd-,
gār-cēne; feor-cȳþþ; un-forcūþ.  (Un-cūþ and wīd-cūþ occur
five times each.)

89
    magu/mago (m.) "son, young man" (prefix) "youthful";
maga (wk.m.) "son, young man"; mæcg/mecg (m.) "man"; mǣġ
(pl. māgas) (m.,f.) "kinsman (kinswoman)"; mæġþ (f.) "MAID-
en, woman"; māge (wk.f.) "kinswoman"; mǣġþ (f.) "tribe,
nation."

The ModG cognate is Magd "maidservant."  The very frequent
mǣġ often means little more than "man."  It is remarkable
that so important a word as mǣġ was driven out of English
by "kin" and the less punchy "relative."
Cpds.:  magu-driht, -rinc, -þeġn; hilde-, ōret-, wræc-mecg;
cnēo-, fæderen-, frēo-, hēafod-, hlēo-, wine-mǣġ "friendly
kinsman"; mǣġ-burg, -wine.

89
    sīþ (m.) "journey, venture, exploit" or "time, occa-
sion"; ġe-sīþ (m.) "companion, retainer"; sīðian (II) "journey"; sendan (I) "SEND."

The verbs sīðian and sendan are related as "to go" and "to
cause to go," i.e. SEND (ModG senden).  The senses of the
group are joined in a phrase like "go and have an interesting time."  Probably related to the Lat. sentīre "to feel,"
by a metaphorical extension of the sense.  Apparently not

related to the adverb sīþ "later" and its derivatives; by
coincidence the groups have equal frequencies in our texts.
Cpds.: sīþ-fæt, -from; bealu-, cear-, eft-, ellor-, gryre-,
sǣ-, wil-, wrǣc-sīþ; for-sīðian; eald-, wil-ġesīþ; on-
"send (away)," for-sendan.


89

    sīþ (comp. adv.) "later"; sīðest (superl. adj.) "lat-
est"; siþþan (adv.) "afterwards, SINCE" (conj.) "SINCE, after, as soon as, from the time when."

ModE "since" is a reduction of MidE sithence < siþþan. Cognate are ModG seit "since" and perhaps Lat. sērus "late."


88

    feorh (n., m.) "life, soul, person"; fīras (m.pl.) "hu-
man beings"; ferhþ (m., n.) "spirit, heart, time."

Feorh is a favorite compounding-element in Beowulf. The
noun fīras is derived from feorh, whose nom. and acc. pl.
form is feorh. To get at a feorh in a military context is
to cut to the quick, the part of a person which makes him
alive (or as we say, inversely, makes him mortal). Wīde-
ferhþ means "for a long time"; for the association of "life"
with "time" see weorold (No. 47), ǣfre (No. 97), eald (131).
Cpds.: ġeogoþ-feorh; feorh-bealu "mortal affliction,"
-benn, -bold, -bona, -cynn, -ġenīþla "mortal foe," -hūs,
-lāst, -legu, -sēoc, -sweng, -wund; collen-, sāriġ-, swīþ-
"stout-hearted," wīde-ferhp; ferhþ-frec, -ġenīþla, -loca.


88

    līf (n.) "LIFE"; libban/lif(i)ġan (lifde) (III) "LIVE";
lāf (f.) "LEAVings, what is LEFT as inheritance, survivors";
lǣfan (I) "LEAVE."

The connection between leave and life, if the conjecture is
right, is in the idea of "remaining (alive)" (see the Gk.
cognate līparēs "persistent"); to leave is to cause to
remain. The IE root probably meant "to smear, to be sticky."
The ModG bleiben (be + līban) "remain" and Leib "body" as
well as leben "live" are from the same root. In poetry the
lāf of files or hammers are swords.

Cpds.: edwīt-līf; līf-bysiǧ, -dæǧ, -frēa, -ǧedāl, -ǧesceaft,
-wraðu, -wynn; un-lifiǧende.


**87**

   lēod (m.) "man" (pl.) lēode "people"; lēod (f.) "people, nation."

Cognate with ModG Leute "people," Gk. eleytheros, Lat. lī-
ber "free." The synonymous and rhyming OE word þēod (No.
74) may have influenced the forms and sense of lēod. From
lēod comes a noun lēoden "language" (cf. ǧe-þēod [and
Deutsch] "language" from þēod "people") which survived into
MidE, and was confused with the OE word lǣdan from the word
"Latin," the language of the learned. Lēod is a favorite
in Beowulf, often making a verse with a national name in
the gen. pl. ("Wedera lēode"--l. 225).
Cpds.: lēod-bealo, -burg, -cyning, -fruma, -ǧebyrgea,
-hryre, -sceaða, -scipe.


**86**

   gūþ (f.) "war, battle, fight."

Obviously an important compounding element, but without relatives in OE, or any descendents in ModE; the word may be
related to Gk. thoneys "murder," Lat. dēfendere "to defend."
Gūþ is not used as the second element of any compound.
Twenty-two of the gūþ compounds are unique to Beowulf. The
word is found in poetry only; words of this sort must have
given the poetry a special, perhaps archaic quality hard to
imitate in ModE without quaintness.
Cpds.: gūþ-beorn, -bill, -byrne, -cearu, -cræft, -cyning,
-dēaþ,-floga, -freca, -fremmend, -ǧetawa, -ǧewǣde, -ǧeweorc,
-hafoc, -helm, -horn, -hrēþ, -lēoþ, -mōd, -plega, -rǣs,
-rēow, -rinc, -rōf, -scear, -sceaða, -searo, -sele, -sweord,
-wēriǧ, -wiga, -wine. (Underlined cpds. each occur 6 times.)


**85**

   æt (prep.) "AT, in, by" (prefix) "with, at."

Cognate with Lat. ad "to, at." ModG zu (with bei and an)
drove out "at." The cpds. with æt- are not counted here.

85

mīn (possessive adj.) "MY, MINE."

Like the other possessive adjs. (þīn, ūre, ēower, uncer, incer, sīn), mīn is formed on the genitive of the personal pron. ic (not counted in this list) and differs from it only in taking adjectival endings in agreement with its noun.

82

helm (m.) "HELMet, protection"; ofer-helmian (II) "over-hang, overshadow"; be-helan (æ, ǣ, o) (4) "conceal, hide, cover"; heolstor (m.) "hiding place, darkness"; hell (f.) "HELL"; heal(l) (f.) "HALL"; ge-hola (wk.m.) "protector."

The root means "to conceal," especially by covering over: cognate with Gk. kalyptein "to conceal"(whence Apocalypse, "the unveiling") and Lat. cēlāre, occulere "to hide," clandestīnus, and cella "cell, room." Gk. and Lat. k often appears in OE as h (centum/hundred; canis/hound; capere/heave, etc.) as described in Grimm's Law. HALL, HELL, HELM are all covered places of a sort; derived from the same root are HOLE, HOLLOW, HULL, and HOLSTER. Helmet is the Old French diminutive of helm, which the French borrowed from German. ModG cognates are hehlen, Höhle, Hölle, Helm, Halle, Hülle "to conceal, cave, hell, helmet, hall, cover." Cpds.: grīm-, gūþ-, niht-, scadu-helm; helm-berend; hellbend, -rūne, -scaða; heal-ærn, -gamen, -reced, -sittend, -þegn, -wudu; gif-, medu-heal. (A good set of cpds.!)

81

giefan (ea, ēa, ie) (5) "GIVE"; giefa (wk.m.) "GIVER"; giefu, -gieft (f.) "GIFT"; giefeðe (adj.) "GIVEN, allotted" (sb.n.) "fate"; gafol (n.) "tribute."

The frequency of this group in our texts is largely a result of the aristocratic practice of gift-giving, by lord to retainers, as the polite means of maintaining a dryht in an amicable spirit of martial zest. A lord is pre-eminently a bēag-giefa. Gafol, on the other hand, the method of buying off Norse invaders, is a term of contempt--not found in Beowulf, which is thought to have been composed before the Viking raiders struck England. The idea of the giefeðe, the donnée or pre-destined, constitutes part of the appar-

ently fatalistic ideology of the Germanic peoples before
the full reception of Judeo-Christian providential thought
(cf. wyrd No. 102). The word ǧiefan may be related to Lat.
habēre "to have," and hence dēbēre "to owe" (<dē + habēre).
Cpds.: ā-, æt-, for- "give," of-ǧiefan "give up"; bēag-,
gold-, māðum-, sinc-ǧifa "treasure giver"; māðum-, sweord-
ǧiefu; fēoh-ǧieft; ǧief-heal, -sceat, -stōl; un-ǧiefeðe.


81
     (ǧe-)sēċan (sōhte) (I) "SEEK, go to, visit, attack";
sacan (ō, ō, a) (6) "fight"; sacu (f.) "strife"; sæċċ (f.)
"battle"; ǧe-saca (wk.m.) "adversary"; sōcn (f.) "persecution, visitation."

To seek out with a vengeance is to fight. The Lat. cognate
sāgīre means "to perceive by scent"; to be sagacious (<Lat.
sagax) is to have a nose for the truth (as to be sapient
is to be tasteful--Lat. sapor "taste"). ModG suchen, be-
suchen "seek, visit"; the Gk. cognate hēgeomai "lead"
gives us "exegesis," guidance out (of perplexity), i.e.
interpretation. The old sense of sacu as a legal strife
developed in meaning as a "cause," hence ModE SAKE. The
ModG Sache "thing" is from the same root; there the semantic development was from a court affair to an affair in
general, a thing (cf. "thing" and Lat. res "affair of law,
thing," and the semantic development of the Lat. causa "law-
suit" to Italian cosa, French chose "thing." In Icelandic,
the þing is the Parliament; in OE a þing can be a judicial
assembly as well as a THING.) ModE "beseech" keeps the
palatalized pronunciation of the ċ of sēċan. The infinitive
shows i-umlaut; the preterite forms retained the original
ō (cf. þenċan/þōhte, þynċan/þūhte, wyrcan/worhte "think,
seem, work").
Cpds.: ofer-, on-sēċan; on-sacan; and-saca.


80
     (ǧe-)healdan (ēo, ēo, ea) (7) "HOLD, keep, rule"; ǧe-
hyld (n.) "protection."

The ModE beholden "obliged" retains the old past participle
form; the sense developed after OE times. Cognate is ModG
halten "to hold"; ModE "halt" is borrowed from French and
Italian (those traffic signs, ALT, in Italy are not just

for English-speaking tourists), who borrowed it from German. One <u>holds</u> a holiday, or one <u>observes</u> it; the sense
of "behold" as "look" derives from this semantic relationship.
Cpds.: <u>be-healdan</u> "BEHOLD, guard"; drēam-healdende "bliss-
ful."


80

    <u>wiþ</u> (prep.) "against, opposite, toward, WITH"; <u>wiðer-</u>
"against, counter"; <u>wiðre</u> (n.) "resistance."

Cognate is ModG <u>wider</u> "against." The prep. is a shortened
form of the rare OE adj. <u>wiðer</u> (cf. Gothic <u>wiþra</u>) which in
our texts appears only as a prefix. A "false friend": the
sense "with" is <u>not</u> common; only later in the MidE period,
probably under the influence of the Scand. cognate <u>viþ</u>, did
OE <u>wiþ</u> take on the "accompaniment" sense formerly the function of OE <u>mid</u>.
Cpds.: wiþ-fōn, -grīpan, -habban, -standan; wiðer-lēan,
-ræhtes.


79

    <u>be</u> (stressed form bī/biġ) (prep., prefix) "BY, near,
about"; <u>ymb(e)</u> (prep., prefix) "about, around, near."

Both words are cognate with Lat. <u>ambi-</u>, Gk. <u>amphi</u>. Be and
<u>bī</u> are related to ModG <u>be-</u> and <u>bei</u>, with the former un-
stressed, the latter stressed in each pair. Usually be
as prefix is unstressed before verbs and unemphasized preps.,
but stressed (often spelled biġ; -iġ is virtually the same
as -ī) before nouns, or as adverb or emphasized prep. Ymbe
reflects the earlier, longer form of the same word (as the
Lat. and Gk. cognates show). For the loss of the initial
*am- which once preceded be/bī, compare OE bā ( + þā >
BOTH) and Lat. <u>ambō</u>, Gk. <u>ampho-</u> "both." The ModG <u>um</u> "about"
is from the same root with the latter part missing. The
very common prefix be/bī- is not counted in this group.
Cpds.: ymb(e)-beorgan, -clyppan, -fōn, -hweorfan, -ēode,
-sittan, -sittend.

78

findan (a, a, u) (3) "FIND"; -fynde (adj.) "locatable";
ge-fandian (II) "search out, test, experience"; fundian (II)
"strive, direct a course (to), desire (to go to)"; fēða
(wk.m.) "troop on foot, infantry"; fēðe (n.) "going, power
of locomotion, gait"; fūs (adj.) (1)"eager (to go), has-
tening, ready" (2)"brilliant"; (ge-)fȳsan (I) "impel, prepare."

Probably the original sense of the etymon of the group is
to go or walk.  Related would be Gk. patos, pontos "way,
sea"; Lat. pons "bridge"--all with a sense of passage.
(Lat. petere "seek" is a less likely kin.)  For the relation
between going and the verb find, cf. Lat. invenīre "to come
upon, to find."  Fēða is not related to fōt (Lat. pedem)
"foot," but the mnemonic connection is inevitable.  ModG
cognates are finden, Fund "to find, discovery."  Fūs, an
admirable word, would now be FOUSE if it were retained in
English; any poet may use it now.
Cpds.: ēaþ-fynde; on-findan; gum-fēða; fēðe-cempa, -gest,
-lāst, -wīg; hin-, ūt-, wæl-fūs; fūs-līc.


78

(ge-)sēon (seah, sāwon, sewen) (5) "SEE, look"; ge-
sihþ (f.) "SIGHT, vision"; -sīen "sight"; ge-sīene (adj.)
"visible."

The IE cognates are unclear:  sēon may be related to Lat.
sequi "follow" or to the same root as "say" (Gk. ennepō,
Lat. inquam "I say"), or these may all be related.  ModG
cognates are sehen, Sicht, Gesicht "to see, sight, vision."
The ending -þ in ge-sihþ is an IE substantive-maker, which
appears as -(i)t- in Lat. (vanitas, veritas, bonitas),
French -ité, ModE -(i)ty, and in several English words
formed from adjectives (health, length, mirth, truth, etc.).
Sēon shows "contraction" of vowels after an original h
sound was lost (*sehan > *seoan > sēon, with compensatory
lengthening).  So fōn "take" and hōn "hang."  Sēon also
shows Verner's Law in the variation of the original *h of
the infinitive and the w of some of the pret. forms (cf.
weorðan, čēosan).
Cpds.: geond-, ofer-sēon; an-, wǣfer-, wundor-sīen; ēþ-
gesȳne.

77

eorl (m.) "nobleman, warrior."

The word became the title EARL only late in the OE period,
when it took on the Scandinavian sense as the counterpart
of the Lat. comes, French comte "count." The Icelandic
cognate "jarl" has been revived as an archaizing term among
romancers and historians.
Cpds.: eorl-ġestrēon, -ġewǣde, -scipe, -weorod; eorl-līċ.


## GROUPS 51-60

77

hild (f.) "battle, warfare."

Like gūþ (No. 86), hild is strictly a poetic word, used as
a high-frequency compounder helpful to a poet in search of
an initial h (it is not found as the second element of
compounds). Both words became obsolete by the twelfth
century, as the poetic tradition on which they depended
faded. Beowulf accounts for nearly half the occurrences
of hild and gūþ in OE. Neither word has certain cognates
in Lat. or ModG. Notice that many of the bases compounded
with hild are the same ones joined with gūþ: this poetic
word-hoard is small and repetitive. Few formulas seem more
OE than "hār hilderinc."
Cpds.: hild(e)-bill, -bord, -cumbor, -cyst, -dēor, -freca,
-fruma, -ġeatwe, -ġiċel, -grāp, -hlæmm, -lata, -lēoma,
-mēċe, -mecg, -rǣs, -rand, -rinc, -sceorp, -setl, -strengo,
-swāt, -tūx, -wǣpen, -wīsa. (Hilde-rinc occurs ten times;
hilde-dēor eight.)


74

þēod (or þīod) (f.) "people, nation"; þēoden (m.)
"prince."

Cf. dryht/dryhten. From the Germanic root of þēod were
borrowed the Lat. and Gk. cognates which appear in ModE
(from Lat.) as "Teuton." The ModG derivative is Deutsch
(<diutisc "people-ish"), the name of the "language of the
people," the vulgar (non-Lat.) lang. of Germany. OE þēod
(and þēode n.) mean "language" as well, but not in our
texts. The only ModE derivative is DUTCH, a word borrowed
from Holland before it became specialized on the Continent
to refer to the languages and peoples higher up the Rhine.

Cpds.: siġe-, wer-þēod; þēod-cyning, -ġestrēon, -sceaða, -þrēa; el-þēodiġ; þēoden-lēas.


73

    fram (prep.) "FROM" (adv.) "forth, away" (adj.) "fro-ward, brave"; (ġe-)fremman (I) "further, do, perform, accom-plish"; freme (adj.) "good, kind"; fremu (f.) "good action, excellence"; fremde (adj.) "foreign, estranged."

The evidence for the connection of the prep. and the adj. is most striking in the Old Norse forms fram "forward" and fram-r "valiant." The translations "froward" for fram and "to further" for fremman show how the senses developed from an original spatial sense of the etymon. The group may be related to the "for" group. Cognate is ModG fremd "alien," set apart from us. ModE FRO is borrowed from the Scand. cognate of the prep. fram.
Cpds.: sīþ-, un-from; fram-weard; gūþ-fremmend.


73

    gold (n.) "GOLD"; gylden (adj.) "GOLDEN"; ġeolo (adj.) "YELLOW."

Related to gold also is the OE gealla GALL, the yellow humour. Cognate are Lat. fel "gall," ModG Geld, gelb "mon-ey, yellow." In Beowulf, ġeolo refers to the color of lin-den-wood, the material of shields. The terms for colors in OE are confusing to us because the OE spectrum of hues was not divided in quite the same way (e.g., their "red" leaned toward the yellow--but see our terms like "crimson, scarlet, claret, burgundy, velvet, mauve, lavender, violet, heliotrope, fuchsia, flamingo, peach, pink, beige"). Even more confusing are the numbers of OE color terms which de-note, not hue (wavelength), but chroma (reflectivity, brightness, quantity of light) or intensity (purity, ad-mixture of white or black, lightness or darkness). ModE also preserves, from OE, the words "dun, wan, sallow, fal-low, bleak, dusky, swarthy, bright, light, murky, dark, black, gray, white," etc. (as well as words like "livid, fulvous, sorrel, roan, tawny, pallid, tan, bay, buff, pale" from Romance langs.) to refer to "colors" which are not strictly hues. Most speakers would consider this set of words rather difficult to define, because we are not accus-

tomed to thinking of color except as hue, in spite of the
rather large non-hue resources of our own vocabulary.  Add-
ing to the confusion are OE terms which then referred to
chroma (e.g., brūn and hwīt, meaning "bright, shining,"
used of BURNished metal [<brūn]) whose reflexes now
(BROWN, WHITE) refer to hue or intensity.  The group of OE,
Romance, and ModE words connected with "black," for instance,
has not yet been straightened out (blæc, blāc, blac (?),
blīcan, blǣcu, BLACK, BLIK, BLINK, BLAKE, BLEAK, BLEACH,
BLOKE, BLANK, BLANC, etc.):  they seem to refer to "black,
white, pale, dark, shiny," like the colorless all-color
of Moby Dick.  (On OE colors see MLR 46 and Ang.-Sax. Eng.
3.)
Cpds.:  gold-ǣht, -fāh, -ģiefa, -hroden, -hwæt, -māðum,
-sele, -weard, -wine, -wlanc; fæt-gold; eall-gylden;
ģeolo-rand.


73
     lēof (adj.) "dear, beloved"; lufu (f.) "LOVE"; lufen
(f.) "delight, hope"; lufian (II) "LOVE"; lof (n., m.)
"praise, renown, glory"; līefan (I) "allow, permit"; ģe-
līefan (I) "beLIEVE."

To hold something dear (lēof) is to believe in it, and the
extension of a LEAVE of absence is a sign of favor to a dear
one.  ModG cognates are glauben "to believe" (Gothic galaub-
jan), lieb, Liebe "dear, love," Urlaub, Verlaub "furLOUGH,
permission," Lob "praise"; kin also is Lat. libet "it is
permitted," and the Lat. term adopted by Freud for the erot-
ic principle, libīdo.  The adj. lēof survives in ModE in
the phrase "I'd as lief" ("I had just as soon") and "live
long day" (= "dear long day"--lēof simply emphatic) in
"I've Been Working on the Railroad."  From lēof + man came
the MidE leman "sweetheart."  The superl. of lof-ģeorn,
"eager for praise," is the last word of Beowulf.
Cpds.:  lēof-līċ; un-lēof; luf-tācen; eard-, hēah-, mōd-,
sorg-, wīf-lufu; lof-dǣd, -ģeorn; ā-līefan; lēafnes-word
"permission."


72
     ac (conj.) "but."
Those who know Lat. are likely to mistranslate this as "and"

(Lat. <u>ac</u> ⹀ <u>atque</u> "and"; Lat. <u>at</u> ⹀ "but").  No derivatives survive in ModE.

### 72

    þanc (m., n.) "THANKS"; ġe-þanc (m., n.) "thought"; (ġe-)þancian (II) "THANK"; æf-þunca (wk.m.) "dismay"; (ġe-)þenćan (þōhte) (I) "THINK, consider, intend"; ġe-þōht (m.) "THOUGHT"; þynćan (þūhte) (I) "seem, appear."

The sense "thanks" derives from an idea of "favorable thought," ModG <u>Dank</u> "gratitude."  ModG preserves, in <u>denken</u> "to think" and <u>dünken</u> "seem," the <u>sharp</u> distinction between the easily confused OE verbs <u>benćan</u> and <u>bynćan</u>. The latter appears in ModE only in the archaism <u>methinks</u>⹀ "it seems to me."  The verb <u>bynćan</u> is said to be the prior one; the notion "to think" develops from a notion of "to cause to appear (to oneself)," presumably implying an idea of imagining or fancy, i.e. making images or phantasms appear before the mind's eye.  The verb <u>bynćan</u> was lost when the similarly pronounced MidE reflex of <u>benćan</u> approached too close in meaning, as "it seems to me" = "I think."  Note the <u>i</u>-umlaut relationships which hold between the vowels of the pres. and pret. tenses of the two verbs (e/o; y/u); the length of the pret. vowels compensates for the "lost" <u>n</u>.
Cpds.: fore-, hete-, inwit-, or-, searo-þanc; mōd-ġeþanc; þanc-hycgende; ā-, ġeond-þenćan.

### 69

    (ġe-)faran (ō, ō, a) (6) "go, FARE, proceed"; -fara (wk.m.) "FARER"; faru (f.) "expedition"; farob (m., n.) "current, sea"; fær (n.) "vessel"; fēran (I) "go, FARE"; ġe-fēran (I) "reach, accomplish"; (ġe-)ferian (I) "carry, FERRY"; ġe-fēra (wk.m.) "companion, retainer"; fōr (f.) "voyage"; ford (m.) "FORD, waterway"; fierd (f.) "army, military expedition."

Cognate with a group of ModG words like <u>Fahrt</u> "journey," <u>fahren</u> "to go, fare," <u>Furt</u> "ford," etc.; with Gk. <u>peirō</u> "I traverse," <u>poros</u> "way, thoroughFARE"; and with Lat. <u>portāre</u> "to carry" and <u>porta</u> "door," <u>portus</u> "port," from the same root with the idea of "passage"; and with FJORD from the Old Norse.  The <u>faran</u> group is probably distantly

related to the advs. _for_ and _far_ (and perhaps even _from_)
and their numerous relatives, all implying a sense of distance traversed, but the groups are kept distinct in this
list.  The p- of the Gk. and Lat. cognates and the f of the
Germanic words are of course classic instances of Grimm's
Law.  The _fær_ of this group should not be confused with
fǣr "sudden, FEARful attack."  Note how often the stems of
verbs, when an -a is added, appear as wk.m. agent nouns
(cf. -_end_, -_ung_):  _fara_, _ğenga_, _flota_, _floga_, _wealda_, etc.
Cpds.: hægl-faru; æt-, of-, oþ-ferian; sǣ-fōr; fierd-ğe-
stealla, -hom, -hrægl, -hwæt, -lēoþ, -rinc, -searo, -wyrðe.


69
    _nū_ (adv.) "NOW" (conj.) "now that."

Cognates Gk. _ny_, Lat. _nunc_, ModG _nun_ "now."  On the analogy
of _nū_ and _hū_ you should be able to translate "How now, brown
cow?" into OE.


67
    (_ğe-_)_sittan_ (æ, ǣ, e) (5) "SIT"; (_ğe-_)_settan_ (I) "SET,
seat, establish"; _ğe-set_ (n.) "SEAT"; _setl_ (n.) "seat";
_sess_ (m. [or n.?]) "seat"; _sadol_ (m.)"SADDLE"; _sǣta_ (wk.m.)
"one stationed (at a place)."

ModG cognates are _sitzen_, _setzen_, _Sitz_ "to sit, to set,
seat."  The Gk. prefix _kata-_ + the cognate word _hedra_
"chair" becomes Lat. _cathedra_ "chair, dignitary's or professor's chair," ecclesiastical Lat. "bishop's seat,"
hence "cathedral"; Lat. cognates of _hedra_ and _sittan_ are
_sedēre_ "to sit," whence many derivatives, and _sella_ "saddle"
(ModG _Sattel_).  In our texts the OE nouns principally refer
to the throne and benches of a mead hall, as the compounds
show.  _Set_ is a causal form of _sit_, common to the Germanic
langs.  ModE SETTLE, SETTEE are derived from this group.
ModE SEAT derives from an Old Norse form, itself cognate
with _ğe-set_.
Cpds.:  be-, for-, of-, ofer-, on-, ymb-sittan; ā-, be-
settan; hēah-, hilde-, meodo-setl; flet-, heal-, ymb-
sittend; sadol-beorht; ende-sǣta.

66

    micel (adj.) "MUCH, great"; māra (comp.) "MORE, great-er"; mǣst (superl., sb. n.) "greatest, MOST"; mā (adv. comp., sb. n.) "MORE."

Cognate with Gk. megas "great" (our comb. form MEGALO-), probably with Lat. magnus "great." The dialect forms mickle and muckle survive. Mickle, with the i rounded to y perhaps by analogy with lȳtel, would yield muckle in MidE, or muchel, with the k palatalized (as in West Saxon) in the south, hence by shortening our ModE form much. Mā also persists in dialect as mo. In MidE, mo often referred to number and more to size.

66

    under (prep., adv.) "UNDER."

Cognate are ModG unter, Lat. infrā "under."

65

    (ġe-)æðele (adj.) "noble"; æðelu (n.) "noble descent, breeding"; æðeling (m.) "noble, hero, man"; ēðel (m.) "na-tive land, home."

That these crucial terms died out of the lang. in the MidE period, presumably under pressure from the French words reflected in "noble" and "gentle," shows the remarkable in-fluence over the lang. of the Norman aristocracy in England. ModG cognate Adel "nobility." One's ēðel is the locale of one's æðelu. The word was often spelled with the rune meaning ēðel in the Beowulf MS. Perhaps cognate with the IE group of childish names for "father" which includes Lat. atta "Daddy," and the Gothic proper name Attila (the Hun). Cpds.: fæder-æðelu; sib-æðeling; ēðel-riht, -stōl, -turf, -weard, -wynn.

64

    bēag (m.) "ring, crown, necklace"; (ġe-)būgan (ēa, u, o) (2) "BOW (down), sit, retreat"; boga (wk.m.) "BOW, arch."

The word "bee" from bēag is now obsolete except in nautical

use as an iron ring around a spar. The original sense of
būgan is "to turn back," hence the idea of fleeing from
battle (the Maldon sense) as expressed in the cognates Gk.
pheygein, Lat. fugere "to flee." The craven sense of the
verb is common, and affects its use in the Dream of the
Rood. Precious metal bowed into a bēag was the poets' idea
of a noble gift; unlike the verb, the noun has noble
associations.
Cpds.: earm-, heals-bēag "necklace"; bēag-ġiefa, -hroden,
-hord, -sele, -þegu, -wriða; ā-, be-, for-būgan; wōh-bogen;
flan-, horn-, hring-, stān-boga.


64
      (ġe-)licgan (læġ, lāgon, leġen) (5) "LIE (down), lie
dead"; lecgan (leġde) (I) "LAY"; leġer (n.) "place of lying,
LAIR"; or-leġe (n.) "war, battle"; -legu (wk.f.) "extent."

Licgan is cognate with Gk. lechos, Lat. lectus "bed," and
ModG liegen, legen, Lager "to lie, to lay, bed (or beer for
laying away)," etc. LAW (<OE lagu) derives from the group,
but was borrowed in late OE times from Old Norse, meaning
"that which is set down" (cf. OE dōm, Gk. themis [No. 99],
Lat. statutum, ModG Gesetz). In or-leġe and feorh-legu
the sense of "what is established" (the fate of war; the
fixed extent of life) which lies behind "law" can be seen.
(Lat. lēx is thought to be related not to this group, but
to Lat. legere "to gather, read.")
Cpds.: ā-licgan; ā-lecgan; leġer-bed; or-leġ-hwīl; feorh-
legu.


63
      lang (adj.) "LONG"; lenġra (comp.) "LONGER"; ġe-lang/
ġe-lenġe (adj.) "at hand, ALONG with, beLONGing to"; lange
(adv.) "long, for a long time"; lenġ (comp. adv.) "longer";
lenġest (superl. adv.) "longest, for the longest time";
langoþ (m.) "longing"; langung (f.) "LONGING, anxiety."

The connection of "along" and "belong" with "long" seems to
arise from the idea of LENGTH of equal dimension as suggest-
ing the idea of parallel accompaniment, and from the idea
of extension in an opposing direction (and-long) as extension lengthwise, parallelism, accompaniment. LONGING is
anxiety caused by one's long distance (in space or time)

from an object of desire.  Cognate are ModG <u>lang</u>, <u>langen</u>
"long, to reach" and Lat. <u>longus</u> "long."
Cpds.:  and-, ealdor-, morgen-, niht-, up-lang; lang-ğe-
strēon, -sum, -twīdiğ; langung-hwīl.


62
    <u>heard</u> (adj.) "HARD, fierce, bitter, strong"; <u>hearde</u>
(adv.) "HARD, sorely."

Cognate are ModG <u>hart</u> "hard" and Gk. <u>kartos</u> "strength."
The three senses of "materially tough," "difficult," and
"unyielding" are all already joined in OE and before.  For
the ModE <u>a</u> for OE (LWS) <u>ea</u>, see <u>eall</u> (No. 159).
Cpds.:  fēol-, for-, fȳr-, īren-, nīþ-, reğn-, scūr-, wīğ-
heard; heard-ecg, -hycgende, -līċe.


62
    <u>māðum</u>/<u>māððum</u> (m.) "treasure, precious object, ornament";
<u>ğe-mǣne</u> (adj.) "common, in common"; <u>ğe-māna</u> (wk.m.) "fellow-
ship, meeting"; <u>mān</u> (n.) "crime, wickedness."

Over two-thirds of the occurrences of <u>māðum</u> in OE poetry
are in <u>Beowulf</u>.  Cognates are ModG <u>gemein</u> "common"; Lat.
<u>mūnus</u>, <u>mūtāre</u>, <u>mutuus</u>, <u>communis</u> "gift, to change, mutual,
common."  The root sense, if the relation of the words of
this group is correct, is "change"; exchange of gifts (<u>mā-
ðum</u>); reciprocation of friendship (<u>ğe-mǣne</u>); change for the
worse (<u>mān</u>).  As the Last Survivor in <u>Beowulf</u> knew, <u>māðum</u>
is mutable.  ModE MEAN derives from <u>ğe-mǣne</u>, and became a
synonym of "inferior" in the same way "common" (<<u>communis</u>)
and "vulgar" (<Lat. <u>vulgus</u> "the people") took on pejora-
tive senses.  The <u>ğe-</u> of <u>ğe-mǣne</u> is the "copulative prefix" seen in <u>ğe-sibbe</u>, <u>ğe-stealla</u>, <u>ğe-selda</u>, <u>ğe-sīþ</u>, <u>ğe-
lenğe</u>, etc., meaning "accompanying," and often implying
fellowship (cf. Lat. <u>cum</u> of <u>comrade</u>, <u>companion</u>, French
<u>compère</u>, etc.).
Cpds.:  māðum-ǣht, -fæt, -ğestrēon, -ğiefa, -ğifu, -siğle,
-sweord, -wela; dryht-, gold-, hord-, ofer-, sinc-, wun-
dur-māðum; mān-for-dǣdla, -sċaða.

62

    (ġe-)wealdan (ēo, ēo, ea) (7) "have power over, WIELD,
rule"; wealdend (m.) "ruler," esp. "the Lord"; ġe-weald (n.)
"control"; wealda (wk.m., adj.) "omnipotent, God."

Presumably from an IE root "to be strong," hence Lat. val-
ēre and many ModE derivatives from the Lat. and Romance
langs.:  value, valence, avail, etc.
Cpds.:  al-, an-walda; on-weald.


61

    hand (f.) "HAND"; ġe-hende (prep.) "near, at hand."

ModG cognate Hand.  The prep. is "post-positive" like many
in OE which have their object preceding them: the fine line
is "hē læġ þeġn-līċe   þēodne ġehende"  "he lay down and
died as a thane should, next to his lord" (Maldon, l. 294).
Þeġn and þēoden are knit in alliteration, and in death.
The ModE HANDY is cognate, but not a direct descendent of
ġe-hende.  Hand is often spelled hond (cf. mann/monn; nama/
noma; dranc/dronc; fram/from; and/ond, etc.) indicating
that at one time a following nasal consonant affected the
quality of short back vowels.
Cpds.:  hand-bona, -ġemōt, -ġesella, -ġestealla, -ġeweorc,
-ġewriðen, -locen, -pleġa, -rǣs, -scolu, -sporu, -wundor;
īdel-hende "empty-handed."

GROUPS 71-80

61

    hyġe (m.) "mind, thought, heart, courage"; ġe-hyġd (f.,
n.) "thought"; hyġdiġ (adj.) "mindful" (suffix) "-minded";
(ġe-)hycgan (hogode) (III) (and II) "think, intend, re-
solve"; for-hycgan "despise"; hyht (m.) "expectation of
joy, hope."

Hyġe and hyht are not etym. connected with the ModE "hope."
Neither important word nor their derivatives are recorded
after the 13th c.; ModG has also lost the group.  In these
cases it seems likely that the requirement in alliterative
poetry for a multitude of synonyms with different initials
for common concepts sustained words in the language which
became obsolete as the alliterative tradition faded.
Cpds.:  hyġe-mǣðu, -rōf, -þīhtiġ, -þrym, -bend, -ġiōmor,
-mēðe, -sorh; ofer-, won-hyġd; ofer-hycgan; bealo-, heard-,
swīþ-, stīþ-, þanc-, wīs-hycgende; an-, bealo-, nīþ-, þrist-
hyġdiġ; brēost-, mōd-ġehyġd.

61

ġe-munan (-man, -manst, -munde) (pret.-pres.) "be
MINDful of, remember"; myne (m.) "thought, favor"; mynd
(f.) "thought"; myntan (I) "intend, think"; ġe-mynd (f.)
"memory, remembrance"; (ġe-)myndgian (II) "reMIND"; (ġe-)-
manian (II) "exhort, admonish."

Cognate with Lat. mens, memini, monēre, mentīre "mind, I
remember, to advise, to lie"; Gk. mnēstis, memona "memory,
yearn," with such interesting relatives as Minerva, money,
Eumenides, mania, automatic, maenad, -mancy, monster. Oddly, the ModE word "mean" (from OE mǣnan "mean, tell, lament")
cannot certainly be connected with this group. The words
in Lat., Gk., and OE meaning "be mindful" are all pret.-
pres. (memini, memona, munan). The OE poets treat the words
of this group as if the ideas of memory and intention which
they imply were of special importance. In these last two
articles and elsewhere in the list, notice that groups of
related words tend to maintain the quantity of the stem
vowel: all these words have short vowels. The "lengthened"
ablaut grade, visible in strong verbs, and other factors,
will disturb their symmetry.
Cpds.: on-munan; ġe-myndiġ, weorþ-mynd "honor."

60

word (n.) "WORD, speech."

Cognate are ModG Wort, Lat. verbum "word," and Gk. eirein
"to speak," hence rhētōr "speaker" (>RHETORIC).
Cpds.: bēot-, ġylp-, lāst-, lēafnes-, meðel-, þrȳþ-word;
word-cwide "speech," -ġyd, -hord, -riht.

59

dæġ (pl. dagas) (m.) "DAY"; dōgor (n.) "day."

An OE verb from the same root, dagian, gives us dawn (MidE
daw). OE g, ġ, often appear as w, y in MidE and ModE
(cf. būgan "bow," mæġ "may"). The group is not cognate
with Lat. dies "day." Chaucer's favorite flower, the daisy,
is the day's eye, like the sun (dæġes ēage). The a in the
plural forms of dæġ is from an earlier æ, lowered because
of the back vowel (a or u) in the following syllable (cf.
hwæl, stæf "staff/staves," þæb, fæt "vessel").

Cpds.: ǣr-, dēaþ-, dōm-, ealdor-, ende-, hearm-, lān-,
līf-, swylt-, tīd-, win-dæg̊; dæg̊-hwīl, -rīm, -weorc; ende-
dogor; fyrn-, g̊ēar-dagas "days of yore."


## 59

(g̊e-)weorc (n.) "WORK, pain"; (g̊e-)wyrc̊an (worhte) (I)
"make, WORK, achieve"; g̊e-wyrht (f.) "deed."

Cognates: ModG Werk "work" and wirken "to effect, feel
pain"; Gk. ergon "activity," whence energy, organ, liturgy,
George, orgy, surgeon.  ModE WROUGHT < worhte (the pret.);
the ModE suffix -WRIGHT (playwright, wheelwright, etc.) is
from the same etymon.  The association of the term "work"
with the idea of distress (cf. labor, toil, travail) is
ancient; we feel medicine "work" in a wound.
Cpds.: beadu-, dæg̊-, ellen- "valorous deed," heaðo-, niht-
weorc; nīþ-g̊eweorc; be-wyrc̊an; eald-g̊ewyrht.


## 58

guma (wk.m.) "man."

Found in poetry only; cognate with Lat. homo, nēmo "man,
no-one" and perhaps with humus "soil," Gk. chthonos "under-
worldly."  ModE "bridegroom" replaced, in the sixteenth
century, the earlier "brideGOME."  "Groom" itself ( = "boy")
is of uncertain origin.  The word gome retains its native
and poetic flavor in MidE verse.
Cpds.: dryht-, seld-guma; gum-cynn, -cyst, -drēa, -dryhten,
-fēða, -mann.


## 58

sele (m.) "hall"; sæl (n.) "hall"; sæld/seld (n.)
"hall"; g̊e-selda (wk.m.) "cohabitor, companion."

Cognate are ModG Saal, French salle (whence SALON, SALOON),
and Italian sala (the French and Italian borrowed from the
Germanic) "hall, room."  The OE words are rarely found in
prose.
Cpds.: sele-drēam, -drēorig̊, -ful, -g̊yst, -rǣdend, -rest,
-secg, -þeg̊n, -weard; bēah-, bēor-, dryht-, eorþ-, g̊est-,
gold-, gūþ-, hēah-, hring-, hrōf-, nīþ-, wīn-sele; seld-
guma; medu-, cear-seld.

58
 sweord (n.) "SWORD."

Cognate with ModG Schwert.
Cpds.: sweord-bealo, -freca, -ġifu; eald-, gūþ-, māððum-,
wǣġ-sweord.


57
 hātan (hēt/heht, hēton, hāten) (7) "name, call, command"; ġe-hātan (7) "promise, threaten"; ōretta (wk.m.)
"warrior"; ōnettan (I) "hasten."

The verb hātan is doubly interesting grammatically. It is
the only example in English of the "middle" or "synthetic"
passive-voiced verb, in its sense "be called": "he HIGHT"
means "he is named" (this use does not occur in our texts).
The only OE forms are hātte, hātton "he (they) is or was
called." It is also one of the few verbs (cf. lācan/leolc;
ondrǣdan/ondreord; lǣtan/leort; rǣdan/reord) which still
show the signs of "reduplication" in their preterites (typ-
ical of class 7), alongside normalized pret. forms (hēt,
lēc, ondrēd, lēt, rēd). Like many IE verbs, these prets.
were formed with a doubling of the stem (cf. Lat. do/dedi).
The words ōret- and ōnettan are related to hātan by an idea
of "calling against" as "to challenge" (Gothic and-haitjan),
esp. a challenge to combat or to a race. The pre-historic
forms of the words, *or-hāt and on-hātjan, show the presence
of hātan. Cognate with Lat. ciēre, ModG heissen "to call."
Cpd.: ōret-mecg "warrior."


56
 fæst (adj.) "firm, fixed"; fæste (adv.) "firmly, FAST";
(ġe-)fæstnian (II) "FASTEN, confirm"; fæstnung (f.) "firm-
ness"; fæsten (n.) "FASTNESS, retreat, place of safety."

The word fæst is used exclusively in the sense "to stick
FAST" in OE. The later development of the word, first as
an adverb, to mean "speedily," is explained when one looks
at the ModG fast "almost, close upon": a fast runner is
one who sticks close to his swifter rivals. Other ModG
cognates are fest, befestigen "firm, to fasten."
Cpds.: ār-, blǣd-, ġin-, sigor-, sōþ-, stede-, tīr-,
þrymm-, wīs-fæst; fæst-līċe, -rǣd.

55

 mǣre (adj.) "illustrious, famous"; mǣrðu (f.) "fame, glory, glorious deed."

The ModG Mär "news, report" and Märchen "fairy tale, legend" are related to these words by a sense of renown; like ġe-friġnan, they hark back to an oral culture. Perhaps also mā and its relatives are cognate. Abstract nouns in -ð are often feminine (cf. Lat. -itas).
Cpds.: fore-, heaðo-mǣre; ellen-mǣrðu.


55

 weard (m.) "guardian, lord"; weard (f.) "watch, protection"; -wearde "guarded"; weardian (II) "guard, occupy, remain behind"; warian (II) "guard, keep, inhabit"; -ware (m.pl.), -wara (f.pl.) "dwellers, people."

Cognate with ModG Wart, wahren "keeper, to watch over," Gk. ōra "care," Lat. verēri "to revere, fear." Perhaps OE wǣre "pledge, protection," wearn "hindrance, refusal," and warnian "warn" are also related. French borrowed from Germanic its word guard (cf. William/Guillaume; war/guerre; wily/guile [?] for Germanic w-/French gu- pairs). WARD took on its sense of "kept" (as a foster-child, like Batman's ally Robin) rather than "keeper" by the 15th c. The OE word hlāford (>Scottish "laird," ModE "lord") and its compounds occur sixteen times in our texts. It derives from hlāf "bread" (>LOAF) + weard; the lord is the guardian of the bread (as the lady, hlǣfdiġe, is in charge of making the bread). Hlāford is not counted here.
Cpds.: bāt-, brycg-, eorþ-, ēðel-, gold-, hord-, hȳþ-, land-, ren-, sele-, yrfe-weard; ǣġ-, eoton-, ferh-, hēafod-weard (f.); or-wearde; bealu-, burg-ware; land-waru.


53

 eorðe (wk.f.) "EARTH."

Cognate with ModG Erde, perhaps Gk. era "earth." In poetry esp., it competed with middan-ġeard in the sense of "world."
Cpds.: eorþ-cyning, -draca, -hūs, -reċed, -scræf, -sele, -weall, -weard, -weġ, -wela.

53

folc (n.) "people, army, FOLK."

ModG cognate Volk.  The original sense may have been the
military one.  Flock--OE flocc--is obscure in origin, but
may derive from this word by an unusual (for OE) metathesis (inversion of letters).  Perhaps related to fela
(No. 97).
Cpds.:  folc-āgende, -cwēn, -cyning, -rēd, -riht, -scaru,
-stede, -toga; big̊-, sig̊e-folc.


53

hwīl (f.) "space of time, WHILE"; hwīlum (dat. pl.
of hwīl) "sometimes, formerly, WHILOM."

"Whilom" had the sense "once upon a time" for centuries.
Cognate with ModG Weile "while"; Lat. quiēs, tranquillus
"rest, quiet."
Cpds.:  dæg̊-, earfoþ-, g̊escæp-, langung-, orleg̊-, sig̊e-hwīl.


53

wæl (n.) "the slain, slaughter, field of battle."

The OE word is now known esp. from Wagner's Walküre, the
Old Norse Valkyrja (ModE Valkyrie) "chooser of the slain,"
one of the twelve war-demons who bore corpses from the
battlefield to the Scandinavian military heaven, VALhalla,
the "hall of the slain."  Like gūþ and hild, wæl is a useful compounder.
Cpds.:  wæl-bedd, -bend, -blēat, -dēaþ, -drēor, -fæhþ, -fāg,
-feall, -feld, -fūs, -fyll, -fyllo, -fȳr, -gæst, -g̊īfre,
-hlemm, -nīþ, -ræs, -rēaf, -rēc, -rēow, -rest, -sceaft,
-seax, -sleaht, -spere, -steng, -stōw "place of slaughter,"
-wulf.


53

wrecan (æ, ǣ, e) (5) "drive (out), banish, avenge,
utter, recite"; g̊e-wrecan (5) "avenge, punish"; wracu (f.)
"revenge, misery"; wræc (n.) "persecution, misery, exile";
wrec̊c̊a (wk.m.) "an exile, adventurer"; wrecend (m.) "reven-
ger."

The Lat. cognate urgēre "to URGE, push, drive" suggests
the original sense of the root of this group. The ModG
cognate rächen "to avenge" corresponds to the OE development
of the sense, but another ModG cognate, Recke "hero, warrior," shows a line of development of meaning abandoned by
English in favor of the notion of exile and torment. The
heroic and tormented senses are nearly joined, however, in
the word wrecča, whose ModE reflex is WRETCH: Klaeber
glosses the word "exile, adventurer, hero"--a man on his
own was potentially a hero. But as the elegies show, the
life of exile was felt to be mainly wretched: few words in
the elegies are as stern as wræc-lāstas "paths of exile."
We can still use WREAK (<wrecan) not only of vengeance but
of an utterance: one "drives forth" or vents his feelings
in speech, esp. by making a poem. At this point the verb is
easily confused with reččan in one of its senses, "to narrate." MidE evidence suggests that a word wrēc (f.) may
have been in variation with wrĕc (n.), but the OE metrical
evidence is insufficient to determine the length of the
vowel. ModE WRECK comes from early French, ultimately
derived from the same stem as WRACK (<wræc).
Cpds.: ā-, for-wrecan; un-wrecen; ġyrn-, nȳd-wracu; wræc-
lāst, -mæcg, -sīþ.


52
     wītan (ā, i, i) (1) "impute, blame"; wīte (n.) "punish-
ment, torment"; wītnian (II) "punish, torment"; ed-wīt- (n.)
"reproach, disgrace"; ġe-wītan (1) "go, depart, betake,
die"; wuton/uton (hortatory auxiliary) "let us."

From the idea of "seeing" which lies behind the related
group witan "know" (No. 96) comes the idea of WITnessing
and hence charging with blame, wītan. Compare the Lat.
animadvertere "to turn one's attention to, to observe, to
blame." From blaming to punishing was a step taken in
several Germanic langs. The very frequent verb ġe-wītan
"go" (always with ġe- in our texts) likewise derives its
meaning from "to see": one looks at a place intending to
to there, and then (perfective ġe-) one goes. The word
ġe-wītan is often accompanied by a verb of motion in the
infinitive, and a reflexive pronoun (Him Scyld ġewāt . . .
feran "Scyld went (betook himself off) carrying"--Beowulf
26-7). From the base of ġe-wītan, the 1st person pl.
subjunctive "let us go" is wuton, often shortened (uniquely)

to <u>uton</u>. Its use as "let's" in general, with an <u>infinitive</u>, may be compared with the French <u>allons</u>. Wītan, <u>wĭtan</u>, and <u>ģe-wītan</u> are easily confused; remember that <u>wĭtan</u> is a pret.-pres. verb. ModE TWIT is from <u>æt-wītan</u> "reproach" by "false division" (the <u>t</u> taken from the prefix and affixed to the base).
Cpds.: æt-, oþ-wītan; ed-wīt-līf, forþ-ģewītan.


51
    <u>hord</u> (n.) "HOARD, treasure."

The common compound <u>hord-weard</u> usually refers to the dragon in <u>Beowulf</u>. Cognate is ModG <u>Hort</u> "hoard." The root may indicate something hidden.
Cpds.: hord-ærn, -burh, -cofa, -ģestrēon, -māðum, -<u>weard</u>, -wela, -weorðung, -wynn, -wyrðe; bēah-, brēost-, word-, wyrm-hord.


51
    <u>maniģ</u> (adj., pron.) "MANY a" (pl.) "many"; <u>meniġu</u> (f.) "multitude."

Like the ModG cognate <u>manch</u>, <u>maniģ</u> can modify a singular noun, where we must translate "many a." Kin to <u>meniġu</u> is ModG <u>Menge</u> "quantity, crowd."
Cpd.: for-maniģ.


GROUPS 91-100

51
    <u>sum</u> (adj., pron.) "one, a certain (one), SOME, some-one, a special one"; <u>sin-</u> "continual, great"; <u>sim(b)le</u> (adv.) "always."

In the U.S. version of ModE the phrase "some men" is ambiguous unless we mark stress: "some mén" means "a few men, certain men"; "sóme mèn" means "unusually interesting men, very good men" ("thóse were sóme tomàtoes"). This latter, emphatic sense is not a direct derivative of OE usage, but it is frequent in OE, especially when <u>sum</u> is accompanied by a partitive genitive:

Næfre ic māran geseah

eorla ofer eorþan,    ðonne is ēower sum,

secg on searwum;    nis þæt seldguma . . . .

(<u>Beowulf</u> 247-9)

"I never saw a greater noble on earth than that <u>one</u> among
you, that warrior in his armor; that's no courtly fop . .
. ."  The OE idiom <u>twelfa</u> <u>sum</u> usually means "one in a company of twelve, including the one," although sometimes it
means "one of thirteen."  If everything is one, conceived
temporally, it is perpetual, and conceived spatially, it is
of vast extent:  so <u>sum</u> in its etym. sense of "one" is
related to <u>sin</u>-.  The cognates make the relationship clear:
Gk. <u>heis</u> "one," Lat. <u>semper</u>, <u>simplex</u>, <u>semel</u>, <u>simul</u> "always,
simple, once, like."  Apparently the only ModE reflex of
<u>sin</u>- is the name of an <u>evergreen</u> plant, "sengreen" (a leek
or a periwinkle), ModG <u>Sinngrün</u>.  <u>Sin</u>- is easy to confuse
with <u>synn</u> "wrong," sometimes used as a prefix and spelled
like <u>sin</u>-.  "Some" is spelled with <u>o</u> for the original <u>u</u>
for the same reason as are "come" (No. 90) and "worm"
(No. 27), which see.  Related to this group also is the
suffix -<u>some</u> (ModE <u>lonesome</u>, OE <u>longsum</u> "long-lasting,"
ModG <u>langsam</u> "slow"), but the suffix is not counted here.
Cpds.:  sin-dolh, -frēa, -gāl, -gāla, -gāles, -here, -niht,
-snǣd.


50
     (ġe-)<u>scieppan</u> (scōp, scōpon, scapen)  (6) "create,
SHAPE, allot"; <u>scieppend</u> (m.) "(the) Creator"; (ġe-)<u>sceaft</u>
(f.) "creation, destiny, allotment"; <u>sceaft(iġ)</u> (adj.)
"possessed of, allotted"; <u>ġe-sceap</u>/<u>ġe-scipe</u> (n.) "creation,
destiny, the SHAPE of things"; -<u>scipe</u> (m.) "-SHIP, state
of."

The compounds of <u>sceaft</u> esp. preserve the primitive fatalistic and passive sense of the group, that which has been
shaped for one, one's fate (cf. <u>wyrd</u> No. 102, <u>ġiefeðe</u> No.
81).  As often (<u>Dēmend</u>, <u>Hǣlend</u>, <u>Wealdend</u>) the group pro-
vides an active and Christian term, <u>Scieppend</u>, the providential and creative God, the Shaper.  A word which looks as
if it is related to this group, <u>scop</u> "poet, singer," is
not related.  Those who translate or refer to <u>scop</u> as "the
Shaper" indulge in false etymology, on the analogy of Gk.
<u>poiēsis</u> "making, poetry."  (The relations of <u>scop</u> are with
ModE "scoff" and its ancestors:  in the primitive sense he
was a satirist--in Icelandic saga, scurrilous derogatory
verses often became elements of feuds.  Cf. Lat. <u>mimus</u>.)
Cognate with the <u>scieppan</u> are ModG <u>Schöpfung</u>, <u>Geschöpf</u>,
<u>schaffen</u> "creation, creature, to create."  <u>Sceaft</u> "spear-

shaft" is probably related to this group, but is not counted here.

Cpds.: earm-sceapen; forþ-, līf-, mǣl-ġesceaft; fēa- "possessed of little, destitute," frum-, ġeō-, meotod-, wonsceaft; ġeō-sceaft-gāst; fēa-sceaftiġ; hēah-ġesceap; ġesceāp-hwīl; dryht-, eorl- "nobility, noble deeds," fēond-, frēond-, lēod-scipe.


49

   sǣ (m. or f.) "SEA."

The relations of this word are uncertain: perhaps kin to Gk. haima "blood," or to the root of OE sīgan "to sink." Note that it is always the first element in its many compounds (there are twenty-one separate words) in our texts. In Beowulf, the hero is challenged about his prowess in swimming. His challenger Unferþ displays his own prowess with watery words, as he varies the term sǣ with a choice thesaurus of synonyms (ll. 506-519): sǣ, sund, wǣd, wǣter ēagorstrēam, merestrǣta, gārsecg, ġeofon, ȳþ, wylm, holm. This by no means exhausts the hoard of words the insular nation kept for the sea (brim, lagu, hron-rād, etc.). At the end of the series, Unferþ adds a set of terms which, by evoking the pleasures of the return to land, suggests the sort of northerners' attitude to the sea felt in The Seafarer:

             ðonon hē gesōhte      swǣsne ēþel
        lēof his lēodum,      lond Brondinga,
        freoðoburh fǣgere,        þǣr hē folc āhte,
        burh ond bēagas.

"From there he sought out his own dear country, the nation to whom he was dear, the land of the Brondings, that fair town of peace, where he had people, and town, and rings." Cpds.: sǣ-bāt, -cyning, -dēor, -draca, -fōr, -ġēap, -genga, -grund, -lāc, -lād, -lida, -līðend, -mann, -mēðe, -næss, -rinc, -sīþ, -weall, -wong, -wudu, -wylm.


49

   weġ (m.) "WAY, route, road"; wegan (æ, ǣ, e) (5) "carry, wear, have (feelings)"; wǣġ (m.) "wave, surf"; wǣn/wǣġn (m.) "WAGON, WAIN"; wicg (n.) "steed."

The group is cognate with the Lat. vehere "to carry" (but

probably not to the Lat. via "way"); also to Gk. ochos
"wagon"; ModG Weg, bewegen, wägen, wiegen, Woge "way, to
move, to weigh (transitive), to weigh (intransitive), wave."
ModE WEIGH comes from the sense of lifting as if to carry;
WAG from the sense of moving (the ModE noun and verb "wave"
are not related, but identical in sense to words from this
group). Wǣg "wave" must come from a sense of a current
bearing across a stretch of water in billows. Wicg is a
poetic word, rare in prose. ModE AWAY is from the phrase
"on weg̊" taken as a single word.
Cpds.: æt-, for-wegan; eorþ-, feor-, flōd-, fold-, forþ-,
hwæl-, on-weg̊; wīd-wegas; wǣg̊-bora, -flota, -holm, -līðend,
-sweord.


48
    þeg̊n (m.) "THANE, retainer, minister, servant"; þēnian
(II) "serve."

Macbeth has kept the word familiar. The original sense was
"child, boy"; cf. the Gk. cognate teknon "child," from an
IE root meaning "to beget." ModG cognate Degen "thane."
The verb shows lengthening of the vowel in compensation
for loss of the g̊.
Cpds.: būr-, ealdor-, heal-, mago- "young retainer," om-
biht-, sele-þeg̊n; þeg̊n-līðe, -sorg.


47
    oft (adv.) "OFTen" (comp.) oftor (superl.) oftost.

Very likely cognate with the ofer group, but kept separate
in this list. Cognate with ModG oft. ModE often is an
extended form, which came into use in MidE for obscure
reasons.


47
    ōðer (adj., sb.) "OTHER, the other, one of two, second,
another."

The word ōðer is always declined strong. It is the normal
ordinal numeral in OE for the ModE "second." (The ordinals
for 1-5 are forma/fyrest/ǣrest, ōðer, þridda, fēorða,
fīfta.) Cognate with ōðer are ModG ander "other" (cf.

Gothic anþar, Skt. ántara), Gk. enioi "some," Lat. enim
"for," and probably with Lat. alius, alter "other" (and
hence with OE elles "ELSE" and its relatives, but the
groups are kept separate in this list).


47

    (ģe-)secgan (sægde) (III) "SAY, tell"; ģe-seģen (f.)
"SAYING, tale."

The OE sagu (cf. Old Norse SAGA), from which the ModE word
SAW "old saying" derives, does not occur in our texts.
Secgan may be cognate with Gk. ennepe (<*in-seque) "say
(imperative)," Lat. inquam (<*in-squam) "I say." Pret.
forms of secgan often omit the ģ and show compensatory
lengthening (sǣde).
Cpds.: ā-secgan; eald-ģeseģen.


47

    wer (m.) "man, male"; weorold (f.) "WORLD."

In The Faerie Queen, Spenser indulges in an etymology of
"world," deriving it from war old "of ancient strife." He
is not far wrong; weorold is from the roots of wer + eald
"old" (in its sense of "time, life"), more visibly in the
Old High German weralt (>ModG Welt "world"). Cf. Lat.
saeculum, which means "the age of man," and developed the
senses of "world" (as in secular, "worldly, mundane") and
"time" (as in the French siècle, "century"). Eald is
treated and counted elsewhere (No. 131). Wer is cognate
with Lat. vir "man, hero," the base of the word "virtue":
notice that because r and w are not affected by the sound
changes described in Grimm's Law, the words wer and vir
still closely resemble one another. OE wer is preserved
in WEREwolf "wolf-man."
Cpds.: wer-þēod; weorold-ār, -candel, -cyning, -ende,
-ģesǣliģ, -rīċe.


46

    bīdan (ā, i, i) (1) "BIDE, remain, wait, dwell"; ģe-
bīdan (1) "live to experience, await, undergo"; bid (n.)
"aBIDing, halt."

The verbs are easily confused with biddan "ask" and bǣdan "compel" (No. 21): the "length" of the vowels of ModE "bide/bid" helps keep bīdan/biddan separate. The ġe-prefixed verb shows sharply perfective sense, the accomplishment of the action initiated by waiting, waiting through to the end, and hence having experienced or endured (often with a connotation of suffering hardship--"I can't abide this weather!").
Cpds.: ā-, on-bīdan.


GROUPS 101-110

46

ġearu (adj.) "ready, prepared, equipped"; ġeare/ġearwe (adv.) "readily, surely"; -ġearwe (f.) "GEAR"; (ġe-)ġierwan (I) "prepare, equip, adorn."

Cognate is the ModG adv. gar "completely, quite." The ModE YARE "ready" is virtually obsolete except for nautical use ("shipshape"); nautical terminology is extremely conservative of old forms (cf. bee‹bēag; wale‹walu; yard‹ġeard; belay‹belecgan; gangway‹gang + weġ, etc.--words otherwise lost from the language).
Cpds.: ġearu-līċe; eall-ġearo; on-ġierwan; fæðer-ġearwe "feather-gear, plumage."


46

*mōtan (mōt, mōst, mōste) (pret.-pres.) "may, be permitted, MUST."

Cognate is ModG müssen "must," and perhaps OE metan "measure" (but the words are kept separate in this list). The ModE reflex must is from the OE pret. subjunctive form; it is a "false friend"--the sense "may" is much more common, and closer to the original Germanic sense of the stem, of "having enough room."


45

god (m.) "GOD" (n.) "god."

The word is not related to OE gōd "good"; cf. OE man "one," mān "crime." Such pairs show the phonemic force of vowel length in OE. The pre-history of this Germanic word (ModG Gott) is obscure.

45

 oþ/oþ-þæt/oþ-þe (prep., conj.) "until"; oþ- "away, off."

The disjunctive prefix is not counted here.  The conjunction oþþe should not be confused with its homophone oþþe "or."


44

 frēogan (II) "love, favor"; frēond (m.) "FRIEND";
frēod (f.) "friendship, peace"; friþ (m.) frioðu (wk.f.)
"peace, safety, refuge"; frēo (f.) "lady"; frēo- (adj.)
"FREE, noble, dear."

The Skt. word prī "to endear" lies near the root of this
group.  The step from frēod to friþ is easy enough seman-
tically.  Those most dear, in a household, are the relatives of the head, not the slaves:  hence the dear are
the free.  Compare the Lat. līberī "children," literally
"the free ones" in the household.  Frederick (Friedrich)
means "peaceful ruler."  Friday is the day of Frigg, a
Scand. goddess who was the beloved lady of Odin (for whom
Wednesday was named).  The pl. of frēond is normally
friend, but the -as pl. sometimes occurs.
Cpds.:  frēond-lār, -laðu, -lēas, -līċe, -scipe; frioðo-
burh, -sibb, -wǣr, -webbe, -wong; fen-freoðo; frēo-burh,
-dryhten, -līċ, -mǣġ, -wine.


44

 (ġe-)niman (a, ā, u) (4) "take, seize, take off, kill."

Cognate with ModG nehmen "to take"; prob. Gk. nemein, nomos
"to distribute, law"; Lat. numerus "number."  The ppl. "tak-
en (with cold)" is ModE NUMB; also derived from the etymon
is NIMBLE, which first meant quick to take in learning,
clever, nimble-witted.  Niman was driven out by "take,"
borrowed from Scand.
Cpds.:  be-, for-niman "take away, destroy."


44

 sunu (m.) "SON."

ModG Sohn, Gk. hyios "son" are cognate.  The word is a "u-
stem" noun with unusual case endings in -a in gen., dat.

sg. and nom. pl.  In poetry the word often begins a formula, followed by a proper name in the genitive.

### 43

ellen (n.) "courage, valor, strength, zeal."

Another heroic term prominent in Beowulf and lost from English.
Cpds.:  mæġen-ellen; ellen-dǣd, -gǣst, -līċe, -mǣrðu, -rōf, -sīoc, -weorc "deeds of valor."

### 43

self (pron.) "SELF."

Cognate is ModG selb; perhaps the initial s is related to the German and Lat. reflexive pronouns sich and se.  The word often has more intensive than reflexive force in OE.

### 43

*þurfan (þearf, þearft, þorfte) (pret.-pres.) "need, have reason"; þearf (f.) "need, distress"; þearfa (wk.m.) "one in need"; ġe-þearfian (II) "necessitate."

Cognate with ModG bedürfen, Bedarf "to need, requirement."
Cpds.:  fyren-, nearo-þearf.

### GROUPS 111-120

### 42

ecg (f.) "EDGE, sword."

A favorite metonymy of the poets.  Ecg is cognate with ModG Eck(e) "angle, edge"; Gk. akmē "acme" (with a sense "pimple," hence acne); Lat. aciēs "edge, point" and with EAR or spike of wheat.
Cpds.:  ecg-bana, -clif, -hete, -þracu; brūn-, heard-, stȳl-ecg.

### 42

hæleþ/hæle (m.) "man, warrior, hero."

Cognate with ModG Held "hero" as in Heldentenor, in Wagner.

Like æðele, a noble word lost from the language.


41
     dugan (dēag, dohte) (pret.-pres.) "avail, be good for,
be strong"; duguþ (f.) (1)"company of tried retainers,
host" (2)"power, excellence, virtue"; ge-dīgan (I) "survive, endure"; dyhtiǧ (adj.) "DOUGHTY, strong, good."

Cognate with ModG taugen, Tugend "to be good for, virtue";
Gk. tychē "fortune." If DOUTH had survived into ModE
(<duguþ) it might have been used, as it was in OE, in
contrast to ǧeoguþ (>YOUTH) "the inexperienced among the
band of retainers" (No. 39), as a more forceful term for
the virtues of maturity than "middle-aged."


41
     feor(r) (adv.) "FAR, long ago"; feorran (adv.) "from
aFAR"; feorran (I) "take away."

Cognate with ModG fern, entfernt "far, remote"; Gk. perā
"further." The group is probably related to fyrn "former,"
and ultimately to for (No. 141), but the words are kept
apart in this list.
Cpds.:  feor-būend, -cȳþþ, -weǧ; feorran-cund.


41
     lāst (m.) "track, footprint"; lǣstan (I) "follow,
serve"; ǧe-lǣstan (I) "serve, fulfill"; lār (f.) "instruc-
tion, counsel, LORE"; (ǧe-)lǣran (I) "teach"; leornian
(II) "LEARN"; list (m., f.) "skill."

The cobbler's LAST is a sort of wooden footprint. Cognate
are ModG Leisten, Geleise "shoemaker's last, track"; Lat.
līra "furrow." (Someone who is delirious has gone off the
track.) If you have followed the track of a subject, you
have learned it: hence the connection of lāst and lār. Cognate are ModG Lehre, lernen, List "doctrine, to learn, cunning." In OE leornian and lǣran have their modern senses
only; in MidE they confusingly retained their old senses,
but learn came also to mean "teach" and lere also to mean
"learn." Now to "learn" someone about a subject is considered bad usage, in spite of its antiquity.

Cpds.: lāst-word; feorh-, fēðe-, fōt-, wræc-lāst; ful-
læstan/fylstan "help"; lār-cwide; frēond-lār.


41

    wīd (adj.) "WIDE, extended"; wīde (adv.) "widely, far."

Cognate with ModG weit "wide." Both feorr and wīd, in their
uses and their compounds, suggest the international character of fame and exile in the heroic and elegiac poetry.
Cpds.: wīd-cūþ "famous," -ferhþ, -floga, -scofen, -wegas.


40

    dēaþ (m.) "DEATH"; dēad (adj.) "DEAD."

It is remarkable that an OE ancestor of ModE DIE, which
should have been dīegan, does not occur in OE texts. The
(Germanic) word may simply not have existed in OE, and have
been borrowed in MidE from Scand. Steorfan, sweltan, forþ-
gān, ge-wītan, etc., did service for it. ModG cognates are
Tod, tot "death, dead."
Cpds.: dēaþ-bedd, -cwalu, -cwealm, -dæg, -fǣge, -scua,
-wērig, -wīc; gūþ-, wæl-, wundor-dēaþ.


40

    þurh (prep.) "THROUGH, because of."

Common as a prefix. Cognate ModG durch "through." The
emphatic stress developed a variant form þuruh in OE, the
ancestor of ModE THOROUGH (cf. burh and borough, sorg and
sorrow, mearh and marrow); the lighter ordinary stress permitted metathesis of the r and the u. A related sb. þyrel
"pierced place" gives us (with nos- "nose") nostril; a
related OE verb þyrlian is the ancestor of ModE THRILL in
its old sense, "to pierce."
Cpds.: þurh-brecan, -drīfan, -dūfan, -etan, -fōn, -tēon,
-wadan.


39

    geong (adj.) "YOUNG" (superl. "most recent"); geoguþ
(f.) "YOUTH, band of young retainers."

The ġeoguþ is the young counterpart of the duguþ in a company of warriors.  Cognate are ModG jung, Jugend "young,
youth"; Lat. iuventa, iuvencus, iuvenis "youth, young man
or bullock, young."
Cpd.: ġeogoþ-feorh.


39
    lēoht (n., adj.) "LIGHT"; līexan (I) "shine"; līeġ
(m.) "flame, fire"; lēoma (wk.m.) "light, gleam."

Cognate are Gk. lychnos, leykos "light, shining"; Lat. lūx,
lucēre, lumen, lūcus, luna, lucidus "light, to shine, lamp,
grove, moon, lucid"; ModG Licht(en), Leucht(en) "(to)
light."  "Light" in the sense "of little weight" (ModG
leicht, OE lĕoht) has a separate etymology.  ModE gleam is
not related to lēoma, but is a mnemonic aid.  Like ecg,
lēoma is used metonymically for the glitterer, the sword.
Cpds.: æfen-, fȳr-, morgen-lēoht; līġ-draca, -eġesa, ȳþ;
æled-, beado-, byrne-, hilde-lēoma.


                GROUPS 121-130
39
    metan (æ, ǣ, e) (5) "METE, measure, traverse"; ġe-met
(n.) "measure, means, power" (adj.) "proper, MEET"; metod
(m.) "the Measurer, God, fate"; mǣte (adj.) "small, moder-
ate, inferior."

Cognate are ModG Mass, messen "measure, to measure"; Gk.
medimnos "measure (of grain)"; Lat. modius, meditāri,
modus "bushel, to meditate, measure/manner."  Probably the
group is ultimately cognate with Lat. mētēri "to MEASURE"
and its numerous derivatives, and with OE mǣl "occasion,
MEAL," but the latter word is not counted here.  *Mōtan
(No. 46) may also be related.  Me(o)tod originally meant
"what is meted out, fate" (cf. weird), and later, "God."
Cpds.:  Eald-metod; metod-sceaft "decree of fate"; un-ġe-
mete; un-iġmetes.


39
    nīþ (m.) "malice, enmity, violence, persecution, com-
bat."

Not a nice word, but a Beowulfian word.  Cognate is ModG
Neid "envy, rancor," which gives the original sense.  In

cpds., often synonymous with gūþ, hilde-, etc.
Cpds.: nīþ-draca, -gæst, -ğeweorc, -grim, -heard, -hēdiğ,
-sele, -wundor; bealo-, fær-, here-, hete-, inwit-, searo-
"crafty," wæl-nīþ.


38
    (ğe-)beorgan (ea, u, o) (3) "protect, save"; ğe-beorg
(n.) "defense, protection"; burg/burh (byriğ) (f.) "stronghold, walled town, BURG"; byrğan (I) "BURY"; ğe-byrğa (wk.
m.) "protector, surety."

The group is apparently unconnected with beorg "hill, BAR-
ROW" (No. 21), which is itself not connected with bearwe
"BARROW," as in wheel-barrow, cognate with beran (No. 140).
ModE BORROW is derived from beorgan, with the idea of giving
security transferred to the idea of taking the loan for
which security is given. ModG cognates are Burg, borgen,
verbergen, burgen "fortress, to borrow, to conceal, to
guarantee."
Cpds.: be-, ymb-beorgan; frēo-, freoðo-, hēa-, hlēo-,
hord-, lēod-, mæğ-, scield-burh; burh-loca, -stede, -ware,
-wela; lēod-ğebyrğea.


38
    hēr (adv.) "HERE"; hider (adv.) "HITHER"; heonan (adv.)
"HENCE."

Cognate are ModG hier "here," hin, hierher "hither" and Lat.
hi-c, ci-trā "here, on this side" (the suffix of citrā corresponds to the -der of hider). The group is related to the
originally demonstrative Germanic stem *hi- (IE *ki-) which
gives us the personal pronouns, "he," etc., not counted in
this list. For the -ce ending of "hence," cf. þonan
"thence." The -s sound spelled -ce derives from an adverbial ending in MidE (orig. a gen. sg.) seen in toward/to-
wards; night/nights ("he plays at night"="he plays nights").
Cpd.: hin-fūs "eager to get away."


38
    land (n.) "LAND."

An old Germanic form, spelled the same way (with the variant
lond) in all the Germanic langs. except pre-Modern German
(lant).

Cpds.: land-būend, -fruma, - g̊emyrc̊e, -g̊eweorc, -riht, -waru, -weard; ēa-, el-, īg̊-lond.


## 38

līap (adj.) "hostile, hateful, LOATHed."

Cognate with ModG Leid "distress"; Gk. aleitēs "wicked man"; borrowed from the Germanic root is French laid "ugly."
Cpds.: lāp-bite, -g̊etēona, -līc̊.


## 38

mæðel (n.) "council, meeting"; maðelian (II) "make a (formal) speech"; (g̊e-)mǣlan (I) "make a (formal) speech"; mǣl (n.) "speech."

Twenty-six times in Beowulf and twice in Maldon we have the formulaic expression "X maðelode": the formula always constitutes the first half of the line; frequently X is a proper name; the verb occurs in our texts only in these poems, and only in this situation. Mǣlan is likewise formulaically used: in our texts it occurs (thrice) only in Maldon, only in the second half of the verse, always in the formula "wordum mǣlde"--"he spoke in words." The group as a whole is poetic; its words are rarely found in prose.
Cpds.: mæðel-stede, -word.


## 38

secg (m.) "man, warrior."

The cognates, Lat. sequor, socius "I follow, companion," Gk. aosseō "I help," if they are actually cognate, suggest the original sense "follower, retainer." The word is found only in poetry (where it is a homophone of secg "sword," another poetic word used only once in Beowulf). It is odd that the Beowulf poet made no compounds of this frequent poetic word.
Cpd.: sele-secg.


## 38

sorg (f.) "SORROW, distress"; sorgian (II) "SORROW, grieve."

Cognate with ModG Sorge "sorrow."

Cpds.: sorg-ċeariġ, -ful, -lēas, -lēoþ, -lufu, -wylm;
hyġe-, inwit-, þeġn-sorh.

## 38

weorþ (n.) "WORTH, value, treasure" (adj.) "valued,
dear"; (ġe-)weorðian (II) "honor, exalt, adorn"; -weorðung
(f.) "ornament, honor"; wierðe (adj.) "worthy (of), enti-
tled to."

Cognate with ModG Wert, würdig "worth, worthy." The weak
verb weorðian is easily confused with the much more frequent strong verb weorðan "become" (No. 102). Weorðian has
the sense "make worthy," esp. by splendid decoration: an
object is ġe-weorðod with gold.
Cpds.: weorþ-ful, -līċe, -mynd; fyrd-, hord-wyrðe; brēost-,
hām-, hord-, hring-, wīġ-weorðung; wīġ-ġeweorðad.

## 38

windan (a, u, u) (3) "WIND, move fast, circle round,
twist, wave" (ppl.) wunden "twisted (as of ornamentation)";
ġe-windan (3) "go, turn"; wandian (II) "turn aside, flinch";
(ġe-)wendan (I) "turn, go, WEND, change."

The pret. of wendan gradually became the pret. of "go,"
WENT. ModE WANDER is from the same etymon, as are ModG
winden, wenden, Wandel "to wind, to turn, change." The ppl.
can be confused with wund "injury, wound."
Cpds.: æt-, be-, on-windan; wunden-feax, -hals, -mǣl, -stef-
na; on-wendan.

## 37

(ġe-)cweðan (cwæþ, cwǣdon, cweden) (5) "say, speak";
-cwide (m.) "speech" (prefix or suffix).

Quoth is archaic now, but we retain the verb in bequeath.
Quote and quota are from a separate root, borrowed directly
from Lat.
Cpds.: ā-, on-cweðan; æfter-cweðende; cwide-ġiedd; ġeġn-,
ġilp-, hlēoðor-, lār-, word-cwide.

37

  (ğe-)feallan (ēo, ēo, ea) (7) "FALL"; (ğe-)fiellan (I)
"FELL, kill"; fiell (m.) "fall, slaughter."

The two verbs are related by i-umlaut, the latter the "causative" of the former (cf. sittan/settan No. 67, sīðian/
sendan No. 89).  The OE noun fiell was driven out in MidE
by fall, based on the verb.  Cognate with ModG fallen, Fall
"to fall, instance."
Cpds.:  ā-, be-feallan; hrā-, wæl-fiell; fyl-wēriğ.


37

  fricgan (defective:  ppl. ğe-fræğen) (5) "ask"; ğe-
fricgan (5) "learn (by inquiry), hear tell"; ğe-fræğe (n.)
"report, hearsay"; friğnan (æ, u, u) (3) "ask"; ğe-friğnan
(3) "learn (by inquiry)."

A group which reflects the oral character of the traditional
poetry.  Forms of friğnan often occur without the ğ.  The
two verbs rise from the same PrimG root; their perfective
sense is distinct and more frequent, as an epic formula of
authority (the poet reports what he hears tell), than the
simple verbs.  Cognate are the Lat. precāre, poscere, postu-
lāre "to pray, to demand, to request"; ModG fragen, forschen
"to ask, to investigate."
Cpds.:  fela-fricgende.


37

  lǣtan (ē, ē, ǣ) (7) "LET, allow, cause to"; lǣt (adj.)
"sluggish, slow"; lata (wk.m.) "sluggard"; (ğe-)lettan (I)
"hinder."

Cognate are Gk. lēdein "to be weary"; Lat. lassus, laxus
"weary, loose"; French laisser "to allow"; ModG lassen, lass
"to let, weary."  The original sense seems to be to permit
something to go, through weariness or laziness.  LATE and
LAZY are kindred words.  In colloquial ModE the verb lettan
is preserved (as adj. and sb.) in tennis, to describe the
net's hindering the ball from free flight; we also have the
legal jargon:  "without let or hindrance."  Since let "hinder" practically opposes in meaning let "allow," it is not
difficult to see why the former verb was let go, when the
distinct OE verbs fell together in sound and spelling.

Cpds.: ā-, for- "leave," of-, on-lǣtan; hild-lata.


37
    līðan (lāþ, lidon, liden) (1) "go (esp. by water),
sail, traverse"; līðend (m.) "sea-farer"; lid (n.) "ship";
lida (wk.m.) "sailor, ship"; (ġe-)lād (f.) "way, course";
lǣdan (I) "LEAD, bring."

As their compounds show, līðan and lād often refer to sea-
passage. The ModE words LOAD and LODE both derive from
lād, with specialized meanings (the former influenced by
lade "load" <OE hladan; the latter a vein of ore, from a
sense of a course of metal running through the earth).
Cognate is ModG leiten "to lead."
Cpds.: brim-, heaþo-, mere-, sǣ- "sailor," wǣg-līðend;
lid-mann; sǣ-, ȳþ-lida; brim-, lagu-, sǣ-, ȳþ-lād; fen-
ġelād; for-lǣdan.


37
    (ġe-)sellan (sealde) (I) "give, give up, offer."

Sellan does not mean SELL: the commercial sense is rare in
OE, and never occurs in our texts. The original Germanic
sense is to offer, as a sacrifice.


37
    weallan (ēo, ēo, ea) (7) "WELL, surge, boil"; wielm
(m.) "welling, surging, flood, turmoil"; wǣl (m.) "ocean,
deep pool."

Weallan and wielm are used metaphorically of surging emo-
tions in the breast, as if the passions were thought of
as liquid humours. The root sense is probably "to roll";
hence wǣl (used of whirlpools as well as of deep waters in
general) and WALLOW are probably connected, and the Lat.
volvere "to roll"; Gk. eilō "I roll." Certainly cognate
are ModG wallen, wellen "to bubble, to wave." Wǣl occurs
only once in our texts, in a cpd.; it is distinct from
wǣl "slaughter," a frequent word.
Cpds.: brēost-, brin-, bryne-, cear-, fȳr-, heaðo-, holm-,
sǣ-, sorg-wylm; wǣl-rāp.

36
    beorn (m.) "warrior, man, hero."

Beorn may be etym. related to bearn "child, son," with
which it is easily confused in any case, or it may be a
poetic metaphor whose original sense, "bear," was lost.
The phonetically corresponding Icelandic word means "bear"
exclusively. (The OED observes that OE eofor "boar" has an
Icelandic cognate which means "warrior, man" exclusively.)
Beorn is found only in poetry; about one-quarter of its
occurrences in OE are in our texts.
Cpds.: gūþ-beorn; beorn-cyning.


36
    fāg/fāh (adj.) "decorated, variegated, shining,
stained."

Easy to confuse with its homophone and homograph fāh/fāg
"hostile, guilty"(No. 35); in fact the words cannot be
distinguished in some cases. Cognate with Gk. poikilos
"parti-colored." The word bears connotations of ornate
workmanship, of the dazzling, or of liquid staining: gold
plating or Roman stone-work is fāg. Thirty-four of the
occurrences, and all the cpds. in our texts, are in
Beowulf.
Cpds.: bān-, blōd-, brūn-, drēor-, gold-, gryre-, searo-,
sinc-, stān-, swāt-, wæl-, wyrm-fāg.


GROUPS 141-150

36
    grim(m) (adj.) "fierce, savage, cruel, GRIM"; grimme
(adv.) "cruelly, terribly"; gram (adj.) "fierce, wrathful,
hostile"; ge-gremian (I) "enrage."

The ModE "grim" is usually not fierce enough to translate
its ancestor. The formula "grim ond grǣdig," used twice in
Beowulf to describe Grendel and his mother, is especially
fearsome sounding and memorable.
Cpds.: heaðo-, heoro-, nīþ-, searo-grim; grim-līc; æfen-
grom; grom-heort, -hȳdig.

36

heaðu- "battle, war."

A poetic word found very rarely outside of compounds and
proper names in the Germanic langs.  There are 21 different
compound words in our texts which begin with heaðu-.  The
other bases (setting aside affixes such as ǧe-, in-, for-,
etc.) which form more than twenty compound words in our
texts are gūþ (32), wæl (30), hilde (25), sǣ (21)--these
four, with heaðu-, always as the first element--and mōd
(22), here (21), sele (21), and wīǧ (21)--as either the
first or the last element.  (These are counts of separate
forms; many occur more than once in our texts.  Gūþ, for
example, the poetic word par excellence, occurs 30 times
in its simple form; its 32 compounds occur 53 times in
Beowulf, and 3 more times in the poems in Pope's text.)
These nine words may be considered the favorite words in
the poetry; it is interesting that six of them refer to
battle.  Other words which vary with gūþ that have ap-
peared in this list are nīþ, beadu, bealu.  Interesting
studies of poetic compounding may be found in A.G. Brodeur,
The Art of Beowulf (1959), Ch. I and App. B.
Cpds.:  heaðo-byrne, -dēor, -fȳr, -grim, -lāc, -lind,
-līðend, -mǣre, -rǣs, -rēaf, -rinc, -rōf, -scearp, -sīoc,
-stēap, -swāt, -sweng, -torht, -wǣd, -weorc, -wylm.


36

lēas (adj.) "devoid of, without" (suffix) "-LESS";
for-lēosan (-lēas, -luron, -loren) (2) "LOSE"; līesan (I)
"liberate, redeem"; losian (II) "be lost, escape."

ModE LOSS and LOOSE are derived from the etymon of this
group, and LEASE "untrue," from an idea of loose in conduct.
LOSE changes from the intransitive OE losian to its present
transitive sense, and presumably is pronounced to rhyme
with "shoes" instead of with "chose"--as it should be pronounced by normal development--because of association with
LOOSE, itself directly borrowed from the Old Norse cognate
of lēas.  The forms of for-lēosan with r show the operation
of Verner's Law (cf. ǧēosan, drēosan), hence ModE FORLORN.
Cognate are ModG los, verlieren "loose, to lose," Gk. lyein
"to loosen," Lat. luere, so-lv-ere "to free, to loosen/
dissolve."
Cpds.:  lēas-scēawere; dōm-, drēam-, ealdor-, ende-, feoh-,
feormend-, frēond-, grund-, hlāford-, sāwol-, siǧe-, sorh-,
tīr-, þēoden-, wine-, wyn-lēas; ā-, on-līesan.

36

searu (n.) "contrivance, artifice, device, skill, armor"; sierwan (I) "plot, deceive, ambush."

A word of admirable or of dastardly connotation:  the reference is to the cunning machinations of the metal-smith
or the elaborate artifice of a traitor.  If the word is
cognate, as some authorities think, with Gk. eirō "I ar-
range in order, I string (as a necklace)," Lat. sero, seriēs
"to join in a row, row or series or chain," the primary
sense may have to do with the forging of armor.
Cpds.:  searo-bend, -fāh, -gim(m), -grim, -hæbbend, -net(t),
-nīþ, -þonc, -wundor; fyrd-, gūþ-, inwit-searo; be-syrwan.


36

þēah (adv., conj.) "(al)THOUGH, however."

Cognate with ModG doch "though."


35

fāh/fāg (adj.) "hostile, inimical, feuding"; fǣhþ(u)
(f.) "FEUD, enmity, battle."

ModE "feud" derives from an Old French word derived from
an old German word from the same root as fǣhþu.  ModE FOE
is from the same group; cognate also are ModG Fehde "feud,"
Gk. pikros "bitter" (or pikros may be related to fāg/fāh
No. 36).
Cpds.:  nearo-fāh; wæl-fǣhþ.


35

rīċe (n.) "kingdon, realm" (adj.) "powerful"; rīcsian
(II) "rule."

The ModE cognate "rich" is a "false friend":  the OE rīċe
connotes "power" without necessary reference to wealth.
ModG Reich, as "The Third Reich."  The Germanic root (Gothic reiks) is thought to be cognate with the Lat. rēx "king"
by direct derivation via the Celtic rīx "king"--this is
unlike the usual, more ancient relation  of OE to Lat.
words, in which both derive from a conjectural IE ancestor.
If, as seems plausible but is uncertain, rēx is related to

Lat. r̆egere "to rule," then rīc̊e is cognate with OE riht
"right" (No. 23--the words are grouped separately in this
list). A suffix -rīc̊ from this group is preserved only in
bishopric. The ModE "riches" has no singular because it
was originally not a plural, but borrowed from the French
singular word richesse "wealth," itself borrowed from a
German (Frankish) word.
Cpds.: cyne-, heofon-, weorold-rīc̊e.


35
       rinc (m.) "man, warrior."

A strictly poetic word. The cpd. hilde-rinc occurs ten
times in our texts; a favorite formula is "hār hilde-rinc."
The word may be related to OE ranc "strong, proud" (which
does not occur in our texts), and more distantly to the
riht group (No. 23), but the relations are uncertain. The
poets needed words with a variety of initials to say "warrior" (rinc, hæleþ, wīg̊end, beorn, secg) or "man" (mann,
guma, frece, eorl, ealdor, þeg̊n, feorh, mǣg̊, æðeling, lēod);
these words have separate histories and distinct shades of
meaning, but the poets, esp. in cpds., suppressed any very
fine discriminations of sense for the sake of alliteration.
If you want to compose alliterative poetry orally, first
acquire a tongue-tip treasury of variants for the terms
"sea, battle, man, weapon, mind, treasure, distress, land,
people and family, lord, to do, to say, to go, to know."
Cpds.: beado-, fierd-, gūþ-, hilde- "battle warrior,"
heaðo-, here-, mago-, sǣ-rinc.


35
       sinc (n.) "treasure, ornament."

A word found only in poetry, of unknown ancestry and without
a Modern reflex. Sinc is recorded only once as the second
element of a compound (not in our texts): its poetic frequency depends on its usefulness in making compounds which
alliterate.
Cpds.: sinc-fæt "precious cup," -fāg, -g̊estrēon, -g̊ifa
"treasure-giver," -māððum, -þegu (sinc-fæt and sinc-g̊ifa
each occur four times).

34

fēond (m.) "enemy, FIEND."

The OE verb *fēogan/*fēon "hate," of which fēond was originally the pres. part., does not occur in our texts.  Fēond
is one of the "agent nouns" like gōddōnd, hettend, āgend,
hǣlend, wealdend, wīgend, frēond "benefactor, enemy, owner,
savior, ruler, warrior, friend"--all masculine nouns derived from the pres. part. of the Germanic etymons of the
corresponding verbs.  The sense "devil" of OE fēond is common, but it became the unique meaning only later.  Cognate
with ModG Feind "devil" and perhaps with Gk. pēma "distress,"
Lat. patī "to suffer" (>PASSION).
Cpds.: fēond-grāp, -scaða, -scipe.


GROUPS 151-160

34

niht (f.) "NIGHT."

Cognate with Gk. nyx, Lat. nox, ModG Nacht "night."
Cpds.: niht-bealu, -helm, -long, -scua, -wacu, -weorc;
middel-, sin-niht.


34

swīþ (adj.) "strong, harsh, right (hand)"; swīðe (adv.)
"very, quite, strongly, severely"; ofer-swīðan (I) "over-
power."

The adverb often has a merely emphatic sense.  The word
sound (healthy, strong) may be related (OE sund), but the
words are not joined in this list.  Cognate is ModG ge-
schwind "quick."
Cpds.: swīþ-ferhþ, -hicgende, -mōd; þrȳþ-swȳþ; un-swīðe.


33

(n)āgan (āh/āg, āhst, āhte) (pret.-pres.) "have, possess, OWN"; āgen (adj.) "OWN"; āgend (m.) "owner"; ǣht (f.)
"property, control."

The post-OE history of this verb resembles that of other
pret.-pres. verbs, in that the pret. subjunctive (āhte)
came to be felt as a separate verb in the MidE period,

whence ModE "OUGHT" as distinct from "owe." The ModE "own"
has developed from pret. forms, keeping the original meaning; but the direct reflex of the infinitive, OWE, has
altered the OE sense. Cognate with ModG eigen, Eigentum
"to own, property."
Cpds.: āgend-frēa; blǣd-, bold-, folc-, mæg̊en-āgende;
gold-, māðm-ǣht.


33
    (g̊e-)fōn (fēng, fēngon, fangen) (7) "seize, grasp";
feng (m.) "grasp, grip."

ModE FANG, the grasper, is the obvious mnemonic aid. Cognate are ModG fangen "to seize" (with frequent cpds. in ge-,
emp-, an-) and Lat. pactum, pāx "pact, peace"--a peace being a compact with one's enemies, and a pact being a thing
secured--Gk. paktoō "I fasten." The OE fæg̊er "fair" may
be related, but the words are kept separate in this list.
Feng is what Beowulf has plenty of.
Cpds.: be-, on- "seize," purh-, wiþ-, ymbe-fōn; inwit-
feng.


33
    oþþe (conj.) "OR."

It is not certain that "or" is a direct reflex of oþþe,
with a final r somehow added in the 12th c. (cf. the cognate ModG oder "or," with similarly inexplicable r ending.)


33
            sōþ (adj.) "true" (sb.n.) "truth"; sōðe (adv.) "truly";
sēðan (I) "declare (the truth)"; syn(n) (f.) "SIN, wrong-
doing"; synnig̊ (adj.) "SINful"; synnum (adv.) "guiltily";
g̊e-syng̊ian (II) "SIN."

Like cūþ (No. 90), sōþ (ModE SOOTH) is derived from an earlier form *sonþ-, from which the n preceding the dental
was lost, and the vowel lengthened "in compensation." This
earlier form more closely resembles the cognate forms, Lat.
sontis (gen. sg. of sons) "guilty" and ModG Sünde "sin,"
as well as the OE cognate synn. The idea of the true and
the idea of the guilty are related through the idea of

emphatically being the one. So the group is etym. related
to forms of the verb "to be," like OE sint (not counted
here), ModG sind, Lat. sunt "they are." The relationship
of "being" and "guilt" is still present, even outside of
the work of Kafka, as was demonstrated by a comedian who,
a long time ago, played upon a politician's motto, "Nemo's
the one," by hinting that the meaning was not that Nemo
would be victorious, but that he is guilty. The prefix
syn- is easily confused with its homograph prefix syn-/sin-,
meaning "continually, great." For instance, syn-scaða may
mean "sinful harmer" or "great harmer." To SOOTHE has
developed its meaning from "to assuage Nemo by asserting
that what Nemo says is true (sōþ)," i.e. to be a yes-man,
from OE sōðian (not in our texts). A sooth-sayer is not
soothing.
Cpds.: sōþ-cyning, -fæst, -ġiedd, -līċe; syn-bysiġ, -scaða
(?); un-synniġ; un-synnum.


33
    wǣpen (n.) "WEAPON"; wǣpnan (I) "arm."

The ModG Luftwaffe may precisely be translated "air force,"
since Waffe, like its OE cognate wǣpen, has a general sense
"force" as well as a particular sense "weapon."
Cpds.: hilde-, siġe-wǣpen; wǣpen-ġewrixl; wǣpned-monn.


32
    frætwe (f. pl.) "ornaments, decorated armor, treasure";
frætwan (I) "adorn"; ġe-frætwian (II) "adorn"; ġeatwa/ġe-
tawa (f. pl.) "equipment, precious objects."

Of course you know the good ModE word TAW meaning "prepare,
adorn" (ModE TOOL is cognate); these words are formed on it,
with the prefix for- in its stressed form (fræ + tawa>
frætwa) and the prefix ġe- (ġetawa, ġeatwa). The words
mean practically the same thing, and bespeak the high re-
spect which Germanic peoples had for good craftmanship, esp.
armor and weaponry. Perhaps cognate with Lat. bonus "good"
(Old Latin duenos) and another ModE word, TOW ("hemp").
Cpds.: ēored-, gryre-, hilde-ġeatwa; wīġ-, gūþ-ġetawa;
here-ġeatu (all these compounds present forms of the same
word); ġeato-līċ.

32

    frēa (wk.m.) "lord, king, God."

Perhaps cognate with the name of the Norse goddess of love,
Freyja, and perhaps also with the for group (No. 141), as
the chief is the foremost.
Cpds.: āgend-, Līf-, sin-frēa; frēa-drihten, -wine, -wrāsn.

32

    g̊if (conj.) "IF."

Cognate with ModG ob "whether." The word is not the imperative of g̊iefan "give" ("let it be granted that" as to mean
"if") as its spelling in Gothic (ibai, jabai) shows: Gothic
for "to give" is giban.

GROUPS 161-170

32

    sceaða/scaða (wk.m.) "foe, harmer, warrior"; (g̊e-)
scieþþan (scōd, scōdon, sceaðen) (6) (also I) "harm, injure,
SCATHE."

The most familiar words from this group in ModE are un-
SCATHED, SCATHing. Our pronunciation with the initial sk
sound reveals that the English word was probably borrowed
from the Scand. equivalent (Old Norse skaða) rather than
directly from the OE (cf. skirt/shirt, from Scand. and OE).
Cognate with ModG Schaden "harm," prob. with Gk. askēthēs
"unscathed."
Cpds.: attor-, dol-, fǣr-, fēond-, gūþ-, hearm-, hell-,
lēod-, mān- "wicked foe," scyn-, syn-, þēod-, ūht-scaða.

31

    geador (adv.) "toGETHER"; -gǣdere (adv.) "together,
jointly"; gǣdeling (m.) "kinsman, companion"; g̊iedd (n.)
"song, tale, speech"; g̊ieddian (II) "speak, discourse."

The OE gaderian GATHER does not occur in our texts. If
we imagine a speaker or scop collecting his thoughts before
he composes his utterance, we can see the relation of "together" and g̊iedd, but the relationship is by no means
certain. The th of gather and together came into English
in the MidE period, from the d. The group may be related

to gōd ("fitting," hence good), but the words are kept
separate in this list.
Cpds.:   on-geador; æt- "together," to-gædere; cwide-,
ġeōmor-, sōþ-, word-ġiedd.


30
    (ġe-)bindan (a, u, u) (3) "BIND, imprison"; ġe-bind
(n.) "fastening"; bend (f.) "BOND."

The ModE words "bind, bend, band, bond" are cognate.   "Band"
and "bond" are variants of a cognate Scand. word, which was
adopted and rivaled the OE bend in the MidE period, finally
driving it out.   In the sense of "company" or of "strip,"
"band" was borrowed into English from French, but the French
words are derived also from Germanic words.   OE bend is now
preserved only nautically or technically, as in sheetbend,
a knot which joins two lengths of rope endlong.
Cpds.:   on-bindan; īs-ġebind; ancor-, fȳr-, hell-, hyġe-,
īren-, searo-, sinu-, wæl-bend.


30
    byrne  (wk.f.) "coat of mail, corselet, BYRNIE."

The word may have been borrowed by Germanic from Old Slavic,
or vice versa.   The ModG cognate is Brünne.   With the less
frequent syrce, byrne is the standard term for body armor.
Cpds.:   byrn-wiga; gūþ-, heaðo-, here-, īren-, īsern-byrne.


30
    dǣl (m.) "part, share, (good) DEAL"; ġe-dǣl (n.) "part-
ing, separation"; (ġe-)dǣlan (I) "distribute, share, divide,
DEAL out, sever."

The ModG cognates Teil, teilen "part, to divide," with their
many cpds., preserve the senses of sharing and distributing
better than ModE "deal"--but ModE DOLE, derived from dǣl,
keeps the old meaning.   Cognate with Gk. daiomai "to share";
if a demon was originally one who, like a beast of battle,
devoured corpses, the Gk. daimon is also cognate.
Cpds.:   ealdor-, līf-ġedǣl; be-dǣlan "deprive."

30

hring (m.) "RING, ring-mail"; hringed (adj.) "formed
of rings."

The iron rings of which ring-mail was made were valuable
in themselves, like any metalwork. For this reason the
armor sense of the word often approaches in connotation
the meaning of the ornamental rings (bracelets and necklaces)
which lords dispensed to their thanes. Cognate with ModG
Ring, Gk. kirkos, Lat. circus "ring."
Cpds.: hring-boga, -īren, -loca, -mǣl, -naca, -net, -sele,
-þegu, -weorðung; bān-hring; hringed-stefna.


30

līċ (n.) "body, form, LIKEness, corpse"; -līċ (general
adjectival suffix) "-LIKE, -LY"; -līċe (adv. suffix) "-LY";
līca (wk.m.) "LIKEness"; līċ-ness (f.) "LIKENESS"; ġe-līċ
(adj.) "(a)LIKE"; līċian (II) "please, be pleasing."

Not counted here are the numerous words with the suffixes
-līċ, -līċe (although these cpds. are counted in the groups
to which the other element belongs), except when -līċ
means "figure, likeness." Our "to LIKE" derives from
līċian, which originally must have meant "to be conformable,"
hence pleasant. During the MidE period the impersonal idiom
"it likes me" (it pleases me) was altered into the Modern
"I like it"; cf. methinks/I think. Cognate are ModG gleich
"like" (cf. ġe-līċ), Leiche "corpse."
Cpds.: eofor-, swīn-līċ; līċ-sār, -syrce, -hama "body"
(the garment of flesh; cf. flǣsc-hama); wyrm-līca; on-līċ-
ness.


30

(ġe-)sprecan (æ, ǣ, e) (5) "SPEAK, say"; sprǣċ (f.)
"SPEECH."

The r began to drop from the verb in LWS: the Beowulf MS
has one example. Cognate with ModG sprechen, Sprache "to
speak, speech," more distantly with Lat. spargere "to
strew" (cf. SPARKLE, diSPERSE), which points to an
original root meaning "move quickly": speech is a scat-
tering of words.
Cpds.: ǣfen-, ġylp-sprǣċ.

30

    ȳþ (f.) "wave."

By metonymy, esp. in cpds., the word often means sea; by
metaphor, it refers to surges of flame or sorrow (cf.
wielm No. 37). Possibly related to the wæter group (No.
26).
Cpds.: ȳþ-ġeblond, -ġewinn, -lād, -lāf, -lida; flōd-, līġ-,
sealt-, wæter-ȳþ.

29

    bealu (n.) "evil, malice, misery, BALE"; bealu (adj.)
"baleful, evil, pernicious."

The word is quite distinct from OE bǣl "fire, funeral pyre,"
but the two words have been confused in MidE and ModE, as
hell-fire is baleful. Bealu is only rarely found in prose;
the noun was originally the n. of the adj.
Cpds.: bealo-cwealm, -hycgende, -hȳdiġ, -nīþ, -sīþ, -ware;
cwealm-, ealdor-, feorh- "mortal affliction," hreþer-,
lēod-, morðor-, niht-, sweord-, wīġ-bealu.

GROUPS 171-180

28

    ēac (adv.) "also" (prep.) "in addition to"; ēacen
(adj.) "great, pregnant"; (ġe-)weaxan (ēo, ēo, ea) (7)
"grow, WAX"; wæstm (m.) "growth, fruit, form."

Chaucer commonly used eke "also"; we have it in the verb
form "to eke out," to augment. The cognates are Gk. ayxein,
Lat. augēre "to increase," ModG wachsen, Wachstum "to grow,
growth." From augēre may come augur, "one who predicts
(increased) fortune." The adj. ēacen is the past participle
of a verb obsolete in OE. The verb wax has been almost
driven out by the use in ModE of its synonym "grow," except
in reference to phases of the moon. (Some doubt the relation
of ēac to the other words in this group.)
Cpds.: un-weaxen; ēacen-cræftiġ; here-wæstm.

28

    gār (m.) "spear."

Rarely found in prose. The PrimG conjectured ancestor

*gaizo- has rare confirmation in the Lat. borrowing gaesum
"javelin (such as the Gauls use)," Gk. gaison. Kin to gār
are ModE GARlic, GARfish, and GORE, the triangular piece
cut from a skirt to narrow it at the waist. The seam made
from joining the sides of a gore is a "dart," from a French
word meaning the same thing as gār. The shape of the head
of the spear suggested these sartorial terms. The word
gār-secg "sea" is obscure in etymology, and is not counted
here (it occurs three times in Beowulf), but it may be related.
Cpds.: gār-berend, -cēne, -cwealm, -holt, -mittung, -rǣs,
-wiga, -wīg̊end; bon-, frum-gār.


28

    -g̊ietan (ea, ēa, ie) (5) "grasp"; be-g̊ietan (5) "GET";
for-g̊ietan (5) "FORGET"; on-g̊ietan (5) "perceive, understand"; ēþ-beg̊ēte (adj.) "easy to get."

The base verb is found only in cpds. Cognate with ModG
vergessen "to forget"; Lat. praeda, praehendere "booty, to
grasp"; Gk. chandanein "to hold." Our verbs GET, forGET,
beGET are from the Old Norse cognates. The sense "perceive"
is like our colloquial "get it" (cf. "catch on, comprehend");
GUESS is derived from the same group with a similar semantic
idea.


28

    hēah (adj.) "HIGH, deep, exalted."

Like Lat. altus, hēah can mean "deep" when applied to the
sea ("the high sea"). It often bears a noble connotation
in OE, as now ("high art"). Esp. in its acc. sg. form and
in its wk. forms (hēanne, hēan) the word is easily confused
with the unrelated adj. hēan "contemptible, base." Cognate
with ModG hoch "high." As often, the final fricative sound
of the word was lost in pronunciation, beginning with the
14th c., but retained in the spelling (cf. though, through,
etc.).
Cpds.: hēah-burh, -cyning, -fæder, -g̊esceap, -g̊estrēon,
-lufu, -sele, -setl, -stede.

28

here (m.) "army, (in cpds.) war."

The ModE HARRY and HARROW both derive from the verb herian/
hergian (wk. II), based on this noun but not found in our
texts.  Christ did not "rake," but he "plundered" hell, as
an army plunders a countryside, when he harrowed it.  The
homophonic ModE harrow "rake" is not related.  Likewise the
homophonic OE verb herian (wk.I) "praise" is unrelated.  A
HARBOR is a here-beorg, a shelter for (or from) an army.
The -er- changes to -ar- as in bark, barrow, marsh, hart
(cf. the British pronunciation of clerk, sergeant, Hertford,
Berkeley, etc.).  The HERIOT is the here-ģeatu, the "army
equipment" a tenant owes his lord.  Cognate are ModG Heer
"army," Gk. koiranos "military commander."  The word varies
with gūþ, wīg, hilde, etc., in the poetry, providing a
convenient initial for alliteration.
Cpds.: here-brōga, -byrne, -flīema, -ģeatu, -grīma, -lāf,
-net, -nīþ, -pad, -rinc, -sceaft, -spēd, -strǣl, -syrce,
-wǣd, -wæstm, -wīsa; æsc-, flot-, scip-, sin-here.


28

lȳtel (adj.) "LITTLE"; lǣssa (comp.) "LESS"; lǣsest
(superl.) "LEAST"; lȳt (n. indeclinable) "little, small number" (adv.) "little, not at all"; lǣs (comp.) "LESS, lest";
lȳtlian (II) "grow less, diminish."

Probably connected with LOUT ( < OE lūtan) meaning "bow
down."
Cpds.:  un-lȳtel; lȳt-hwōn.


28

nēah (adv., prep.) "near, NIGH"; nēan (adv.) "from
near, near"; (ģe-)nǣ́ģan (I) "approach, address, attack."

The comp. (nēar) and superl. (nīehsta) of nēah >ModE NEAR
and NEXT; the former drove out NIGH, now archaic.  Cognate
with ModG nah, nahen "near, to approach."


28

sefa (wk.m.) "mind, heart, spirit."

The Middle High German beseben means "to perceive," so the

original reference of the noun may be to a faculty of cog-
nition rather than a physical organ; perhaps cognate with
Lat. sapere, sapor "to perceive, taste." Remember that
the intervocalic f is voiced to sound like v.
Cpd.: mōd-sefa (sefa occurs 18 times, mōd-sefa 10)


28
    þīn (possessive adj.) "THINE, THY."

The second person sg. possessive adj., originally the
genitive of the pronoun þū "THOU," but taking strong adj.
case endings (cf. mīn No. 85). Cognate with ModG dein
"thy," Lat. tū "thou."


28
    weal(l) (m.) "WALL."

Borrowed by several West Germanic langs. from the Lat.
vallum, which has the military sense still preserved in
ModG Wall "rampart." The West Saxon spelling shows characteristic "breaking"; in Anglian the word is spelled wall,
the direct ancestor of the modern word.
Cpds.: weall-clif, -steall; bord-, eorþ-, sǣ-, scild-
weall.


                        GROUPS 181-190
27
    bana (wk.m.) "slayer, murderer"; benn (f.) "wound."

The ModE reflex is BANE.
Cpds.: bon-gār; ecg-, feorh-, gāst-, hand-, mūþ-bana; ben-
ġeat; feorh-, sex-benn.


27
    (ġe-)hweorfan (ea, u, o) (3) "turn, go, move about";
hwierfan (I) "move about"; hwyrft (m.) "turning, motion."

The OE hwearf, a cognate word not in our texts, means
"crowd" and also WHARF, both presumably from an idea of the
reciprocal, eddying movement described by hweorfan. Cognate
is ModG werben "to publicize, solicit." In "The Seafarer"

hweorfan describes the wheeling course of a mind flying forth like a bird.
Cpds.: æt-, ġeond-, ond-, ymbe-hweorfan; ed-hwyrft.


27

wundor (n.) "WONDER."

ModG Wunder is cognate. A West Germanic word of unknown origin.
Cpds.: wundor-fæt, -bebod, -dēaþ, -līċ, -māððum, -sīon, -smiþ; hand-, nīþ-, searo-wundor.


27

wyrm (m.) "serpent, snake, WORM."

In Beowulf the dragon is called wyrm as well as draca (the latter a Latin borrowing); in early English the word usually refers to a larger creature than a worm. Cognate are ModG Wurm, Lat. vermis "worm." As with OE wer/Lat. vir, Grimm's Law does not affect the sounds of the Lat. cognate, so it still closely resembles the English (ModE vermin of course is borrowed from Romance). For the o spelling of ModE "worm" see cuman (No. 90) and cf. wonder, worse, wolf, wort--all with historical u vowels.
Cpds.: wyrm-cynn, -fāh, -hord, -līca.


26

heofon (m.) "HEAVEN."

Note the voiced f between vowels, which makes this word (like ofer, lufu, etc.) closer to ModE pronunciation than it appears. The Scand. and High German word of equivalent meaning which appears as ModG Himmel has no obvious relation to heofon.
Cpds.: heofon-līċ, -rīċe.


26

slēan (slōg, slōgon, slæġen) (6) "strike, SLAY"; ġe-slēan (6) "achieve by striking, win"; -sleaht/-slieht (m. or n.) "SLAUGHTER, blow."

The sense of slēan, a "contracted verb," is more often "strike" than "slay." Cognate is ModG schlagen "to strike." Related are ModE SLY (cunning, able to strike), and similarly "SLEIGHT (of hand)," and "SLEDGE (hammer)," and the weaver's SLAY, with which he strikes the weft down.
Cpds.: be-, of-slēan; ģe-, on-slieht; wæl-sleaht.

### 26

wæter (n.) "WATER"; wǣta (wk.m.) "moisture, WEThess."

Cognate with ModG Wasser, ·Gk. hydor (as in hydroplane, etc.) "water," Lat. unda "wave." WASH and OTTER are ultimately cognate, and probably winter (the wet season), but this last (No. 23) is not a sure enough relation to count here.
Cpds.: wæter-eģesa, -ȳþ.

### 25

folde (wk.f.) "earth, ground"; feld (m.) "FIELD."

One of the best verses in Beowulf varies and abbreviates "fyrģenstrēam/under næssa ģenipu" ("a mountain-stream under the dark places of the cliffs"). It is "flōd under foldan," which by its linked sounds seems to reflect a link of water and earth, at Grendel's mere (l. 1361). The ModG cognate of feld has the same spelling and meaning. The words may possibly be related to flett "floor, hall," flōr "floor," and folm(e) "hand," which all occur in our texts, but the etymologies are too uncertain for the words to be counted here.
Cpds.: fold-bold, -būend, -weģ; wæl-feld.

### 25

īren (n.) "sword, IRON"; īren (adj.) "of iron"; īsern- "iron."

The sense "sword" appears by the familiar metonymy (cf. hilde-lēoma, ecg, hring-mǣl, lāf, gūþ-wine). Cognate ModG Eisen "iron": the r appears only in English, of the Germanic and Celtic langs. in which the word is found (the root may be related to Lat. īra IRE). Oddly, the more poetic OE form with r drove out the more prosaic OE form with s in the MidE period, whereas prose forms usually

drive out poetic ones.  The r of īren looks like a product
of Verner's Law (cf. čēosan/coren) but it is probably not,
so "the rhotacism is obscure" (Gk. rho = r).
Cpds.: īren-bend, -byrne, -heard, -þrēat; eal-, hring-
īren; īsern-byrne, -scūr.


25
     twēġen (m.), twā (f.), tū (n.) "TWO, TWAIN"; twēone
(be . . . twēonum) "BETWEEN"; twēo (wk.m.) "doubt"; ġe-
twǣman (I) "separate"; to-twǣman (I) "divide in two"; ġe-
twǣfan (I) "separate"; twelf "TWELVE."

As genders lost their distinctions, the separate forms of
twēġen in English became redundant, and twā (>TWO) took
over the regular uses.  "Doubt" arises when two choices
are present; cf. the cognate ModG Zweifel "doubt" (ModG
zwei "two").  Twelve (Gothic twa-lif) probably means
"(with) two left (over from ten)," ModG zwölf.  Cognate
with twēġen are most IE words meaning "two": Gk., Lat.
duo.  The OE "dual" pronouns wit, ġit may derive their
final t's from the "two" group.
Cpd.: bū-tū "both."

25
     wiht (f., n.) "creature, anything, AUGHT" (adv.) "at
all" (ne wiht = "NAUGHT, not a WHIT").

The ModE WIGHT is archaic.  The ModG cognate Wicht has a
slightly diminutive sense, "creature, infant"; the cognates
in other Germanic langs. often refer to demons or elves.
AUGHT, "anything at all," is from ā-wiht, "ever a whit."
U.S. speakers use "ought" to mean "zero"; "an ought" is
"a nought" falsely divided, from OE nowiht, "nothing."
Cpds.: ō-, ā-wiht/āht, æl-wiht.


24
     bord (n.) "shield."

The mnemonic connection of bord with ModE BOARD is inevitable; the OE word probably is a metonymic sense of the
word for "board."  Or it may be a metonymic sense of a

homophone, another OE bord which had fallen into the same
gender, meaning "border, ship-BOARD, rim." The last sense
could allow the reference to "shield"--a sense of bord
found only in poetry. Probably the Anglo-Saxons knew as
little as we which word was the origin of the poetic metonymy, because the confusion of originally separate genders
indicates that the words were beginning to be confused in
OE times. Cognate with ModG Bort "board" or Bord "border."
Cpds.: bord-hæbbende, -hrēoða, -rand, -weall, -wudu; hilde-,
wīg-bord.

24

       cræft (m.) "strength, power, skill, cunning, CRAFT";
cræftig (adj.) "strong, skilled."

The ModG cognate Kraft "power" preserves the primary sense
of the word; the ModE senses of skill and cunning, and of
one's trade, are not usual in OE (and these senses are
peculiar to English of the Germanic langs.).
Cpds.: gūþ-, leoðo-, mægen-, nearo-, wīg-cræft; ēacen-,
lagu-, lēoþ-, wīg-cræftig.

24

       fæder (m.) "FATHER."

The classic example of Grimm's Law:  Skt. pitár, Gk. patēr,
Lat. pater, Gothic fadar, ModG Vater. The medial d
changed to th in English around the 15th c.; cf. gather,
hither, together, weather, with th for earlier d.
Cpds.: ǣr-, eald-, hēah-, wuldor-fæder; fæder-æðelu;
fæderan-mǣg; suhter-ğefæderan.

24

       (ğe-)hīeran (I) "HEAR, obey, perceive."

To hear docilely is to be apt to obey. Cognate with ModG
hören, gehören, gehorsam "to hear, to belong to, obedient."
Perhaps cognate with the scēawian group just below.

24

       scēawian (II) "look at, examine, see"; ğe-scēawian (II)

"SHOW"; lēas-scēawere (m.) "deceitful observer, spy";
scīene (adj.) "beautiful."

The sense "show," even of the ġe- prefixed verb, is rare
in OE; not until the early MidE period did the word devel-
op its modern causative meaning (cause to see = show).
Cognate are Gk. thyo-skoos, koein "observer of sacrifices,
to observe"; Lat. cavēre "to beware"; ModG schauen "look."
Scīene (spelled scȳne in Beowulf) >ModE SHEEN; cognate
ModG schön "beautiful." The verb is frequent in Beowulf;
the wise warriors seem always to be looking things over
carefully.
Cpd.: ġeond-scēawian.


23
     (ġe-)cēosan (cēas, curon, coren) (2) "CHOOSE, taste,
try"; cyst (f.) "choicest one, the best, (in cpds.) picked
company, virtue"; costian (II) "try, make trial of."

The original sense of this group involved trying out, or
having a taste of something.  Cognate are Gk. geysein,
Lat. gustāre "to taste," ModG kosten "to try, taste."  The
translation of cyst as "choice," with the idea "select,
premium" (as in our quality-grade of meat), is happy, because the word CHOICE, borrowed by English from Old French,
was ultimately derived from a Germanic relative (like Gothic
kausjan) of the ancestor of cēosan (Gothic kiusan).  On
the other hand, ModE "cost" (to have a certain price) is
not Germanic in origin, but derived from a Latin idiom
with constāre "stand at a price."  Verner's Law describes
the voicing of the medial s in the strong verb to z, and
a regular West Germanic shift altered z to r, before OE
times.
Cpds.: ēored-, gum-, hilde-cyst.


23
     (ġe-)drēosan (drēas, druron, droren) (2) "fall, de-
cline, fail"; drēor (m., n.) "blood"; drēoriġ (adj.)
"bloody, sad"; drysmian (II) "become gloomy."

Some scholars doubt that the two senses of drēoriġ denote
the same word, but the semantic relation is easy enough.
ModG cognate traurig "sad."  The ModE reflex DREARY has

lost the connotation of battle suffering, wounds.  Blood,
of course, is what falls.  Possibly drūsian "stagnate" (>
DROWSE) is related, but it is not counted here.  Only drēosan of this group is found outside of poetry.
Cpds.:  bedroren; drēor-fāh; heoro-, sāwul-, wæl-drēor;
drēorig̊-hlēor; heoro-, sele-drēorig̊.


23
    ende (m.) "END, boundary"; endian (II) "END."

Cognate with ModG Ende, with the same meaning.  The ultimate
relations of the word are complex: the idea of boundary
leads to the idea of the thing lying opposite, hence (perhaps) the common OE prefix and- "opposite, counter, against"
(ModG ent-, a privative or negative prefix, like Lat.-ModE
de- as in "defuse, decelerate, demythologize").  The conjunction and/ond and the prefix and- may be related, but
the words are not counted in this list.  The conjunction,
spelled ond when it is not abbreviated with the usual mark
shaped like a figure 7 ("Tyronian et"), occurs 311 times in
Beowulf, by Klaeber's count.  Related ultimately are Gk.
anti "against," Lat. ante, anterior "before, anterior."
Cpds.:  ende-dæg̊, -dōgor, -lāf, -lēan, -lēas, -sǣta, -stæf;
woruld-ende.


23
    grund (m.) "GROUND, bottom, plain, land."

Cognate with ModG Grund "ground," and perhaps related to
OE grindan "GRIND," but the verb is not counted here.  It
has been suggested that the name Grendel is cognate, but
the derivation is disputed.
Cpds.:  grund-būend, -hyrde, -lēas, -wong, -wyrg̊en; eormen-,
mere-, sǣ-grund.


GROUPS 201-210
23
    hræd- (adj.) "quick, swift, hasty"; hræðe (adv.)
"quickly, soon."

ModE RATHER is the reflex of the comp. hræðor of hræðe,
"more quickly" >"more willingly."  Hræd- is only found in

cpds. in our texts.
Cpds.: hræd-līċe, -wyrde.


23

rǣd (m.) "advice, counsel, help, benefit"; rǣdan (ē,
ē, æ) (7) (or wk. I) "counsel, provide for, rule, possess";
ġe-rǣdan (I) "decide"; Rǣdend (m.) "Ruler (God)"; ġe-rǣd
(adj.) "skillful, apt."

In ModE the archaic spelling REDE is often used for the OE
sense "give counsel," to distinguish the verb from READ, the
newer spelling of the same word, meaning "read a text."
Only English and Old Icelandic, of this common Germanic
group, have the sense "read a text," presumably from a
sense of "explain something obscure." Richard (II) the
Redeless and Æthelred the Unready were ill-advised kings,
not tardy ones; ModE READY is more distantly related to
rǣd. Rǣdan was a "reduplicating" verb, showing a pret.
rēord alongside rēd; it coalesced in many forms with a
weak verb of similar meaning. ModG Rat, raten, gerade,
bereit "advice, to advise, direct, ready." Rǣd may be
cognate with a number of other words, if the IE ar-1 group
is a single etym. group: art, inert, harmony, arms, arm,
ratio, rite.
Cpds.: rǣd-bora; an-, folc-, fæst-rǣd; sele-, weorod-rǣdend.


23

riht (n.) "RIGHT, privilege, correctness" (adj.)
"right, proper"; rihte (adv.) "rightly"; ġe-rihtan (I)
"direct."

See rīċe (No. 35) and rinc (No. 35). Cognate with ModG
Recht, richtig "right," Gk. orektos, Lat. rectus "stretched
out, straight." To make things more difficult, the word
may be related to reċċan "to narrate" and racu "recounting,"
and, less likely and more distantly, to reċċan "to care for"
and (ġe-)rǣċan "to REACH." None of these possible relations is counted here.
Cpds.: ēðel-, folc-, land-, un-, word-, upp-riht; æt-, un-
rihte; wiðer-ræhtes.


23

sigor (m.) "victory"; siġe- "victory, victorious,

glorious."

The prefix is frequent in a military sense; to speak of
the Cross as a sige-bēam emphasizes the paradox.  Cognate
with ModG Sieg, "victory," familiar to English speakers as
part of the Nazi salute, Gk. echō "I possess."
Cpds.:  sige-bēam, -drihten, -ēadiğ, -folc, -hrēþ, -hrēðiğ,
-hwīl, -lēas, -rōf, -þēod, -wǣpen; sigor-ēadiğ, -fæst;
hrēþ-, wīğ-sigor.


23

   weorod (n.) "band of men, company, troop."

Perhaps related to OE wer "man" (No. 47) or wer(e) "troop."
Cpds.:  eorl-, flet-, heorþ-weorod; weorod-rǣdend.


23

   winter (n.) "WINTER, (in plural) years"; syfan-wintre
(adj.) "seven-year-old."

The meaning "year" persists, in poetry esp., to the modern
period.  ModG Winter.  See wæter (No. 26).  The cpds. reflect what the Anglo-Saxons thought of it.
Cpds.:  winter-čeald, -čeariğ.


22

   āg-lǣca/āg-lǣca (wk.m.) "monster, fiend, warrior";
āg-lǣc-wīf (n.) "female monster" (i.e., Grendel's mother).

Of unknown etymology; used only in poetry.  In Beowulf the
word is occasionally used of men as well as monsters.


22

   beorht (adj.) "BRIGHT, splendid"; beorhte (adv.)
"brightly"; beorhtian (II) "sound clearly or loud."

The aural sense of the verb is comparable to the sense
"battle-resounding" of heaðo-torht ("-bright") in Beowulf,
or the visual and aural senses of the Lat. argūtus "clear,
shrill."  Probably from the same root is the tree-name
BIRCH (of bright bark); perhaps also breğdan "move quickly
(flash), brandish" >BRAID.
Cpds.:  sadol-, wlite-beorht.

22

    drēam (m.) "joy, festivity, noisy merriment, bliss, music-making."

It is not certain that drēam is identical with the ancestor of the ModE DREAM.  The Germanic cognates of the latter, e.g. ModG Traum "dream," often have the sense of "sleeping vision"; the origin of the meaning "noisy merriment," if the two words are one, is uncertain.  Apparent cognates of drēam in other IE langs. mean "shout."  Old Norse influence in MidE may have affected the sense of the English word, or the OE word may have been lost and replaced, or the sense "sleeping vision" may independently have risen from the sense "pleasure."  Studies of the word may be found in PMLA 46 and Rev. Engl. Stud. 25.
Cpds.:  drēam-healdende, -lēas; glēo-, gum-, medu-, mon-, sele-drēam.


22

    eard (m.) "land, homeland, estate, country"; eardian (II) "dwell, inhabit."

Apparently not cognate with eorðe (No. 53), but probably cognate with Gk. aroein, Lat. arāre "to plow."  The verb "to EAR" (to plow) < OE erian survived into the ModE period (Shakespeare).
Cpds.:  eard-ġeard, -lufu, -stapa.


GROUPS 211-220

22

    flōd (m. or n.) "FLOOD, current, sea"; flōwan (ēo, ēo, ō) (7) "FLOW."

Cognate with ModG Flut "flood," and with Gk. ploein "to swim," Lat. plōrāre, pluit "to weep, it rains."
Cpds.:  flōd-weġ, -ȳþ; mere-flōd.


22

    gāst/gǣst (m.) "soul, GHOST, demon."

Cognate with ModG Geist "spirit, mind, sprite."  The word may originally derive from terms meaning "anger," ultimately "tear to pieces."  The word is easy to confuse with

OE ğiest "stranger, guest" (Lat. hostis), which is sometimes spelled (with a short vowel) gæst. GHASTly and
aGHAST are cognate.
Cpds.: ellen-, ellor- "alien spirit," ğeōsceaft-, wæl-
gæst; gæst-līč, -bona.

## 22

ğeond (prep.) "through, throughout, over" (prefix)
"over, through, thoroughly."

Cognate with ModE YOND, YON, beYOND, and ModG jener "that
(one)."
Cpds.: ğeond-brædan, -hweorfan, -scēawian, -sēon, -þenčan,
-wlītan.

## 22

ğiet(a) (adv.) "YET, still"; þā-ğiet (adv.) "still,
further."

The anterior etymology is obscure.

## 22

ūt (adv.) "OUT"; ūtan (adv.) "from without."

Cognate with ModG aus "from, out of," Lat. us-que "up to."
Cpds.: ūt-fūs, -weard; ūtan-weard.

## 22

wudu (m.) "WOOD, tree, forest."

Often used in a transferred sense for a ship or the Cross
or a spear.
Cpds.: wudu-rēc; bǣl-, bord-, gomen-, heal-, holt-, mæğen-,
sǣ-, sund-, þrec-wudu.

## 21

beorg (m.) "hill, (grave-)mound, BARROW."

Cognate with ModG Berg "mountain" and ModE "iceBERG, BURGun-
dy"; see beorgan "protect" (No. 38). May be cognate with
Lat. fortis (Old Lat. forctus) "strong"(>FORTITUDE).
Cpd.: stān-beorg.

21
    (ǧe-)biddan (æ, ǣ, e) (5) "BID, request, exhort, pray";
(ǧe-)bǣdan (I) "compel, oppress."

Easy to confuse with bēodan (ēa, u, o) (2) "offer, announce,
command, foreBODE"; the two words mingled forms in later
English. Cognate are ModG bitten, Gebet, Bitte "to request,
prayer, petition." The related OE word bedu (f.) "prayer"
gives us BEAD, originally a prayer, then the pearl-like
objects with which prayers were counted: to bid one's
beads is to pray one's prayers. (Old Norse knē-beðr is a
cushion for kneeling.) The relation of bǣdan to biddan
is by no means certain; the obviously similar meaning is
the only real evidence of their kinship (the verbs are
baidjan and bidjan in Gothic).


21
    flēon (flēah, flugon, flogen) (2) "FLEE"; flēam (m.)
"flight, escape"; flīema (wk.m.) "escaper"; ǧe-flīeman (I)
"put to flight, rout."

Flēon is not etym. connected with flēogan (2) "FLY (in
air)," floga "flyer," flyht "FLIGHT (in air)," but the two
groups were confused even in OE because of the likeness
of forms and sense. In ModE the verb fly can mean "pass
through the air" or "escape," but the verb now distinguishes
the senses in the prets. flew and fled. Cognate with ModG
fliehen, Flucht "to flee, escape."
Cpds.: be-, ofer-flēon; here-flīema; ā-flīeman.


21
    frōd (adj.) "old, wise."

A chiefly poetic word, regrettably without descendents,
which means old and wise at once. Cognate with Gothic
fraþi "understanding."
Cpds.: in-, un-frōd.


GROUPS 221-227

21
    hāliǧ (adj.) "HOLY"; hālga (m.sb.wk.) "saint"; hāl
(adj.) "WHOLE, unhurt, HALE"; hǣlan (I) "HEAL, save";

Hǣlend (m.) "Savior"; hǣl (n.) "well-being, HEALth, good luck, (good) omen"; hǣlo (f.) "prosperity, luck."

Health, wholeness, and sanctity are synonymous in the Germanic langs. Our salute hail! (ModG Heil!--see sigor No. 23) represents a wish for well-being (wes hāl! >WAS-SAIL "be well"), cf. Lat. vale (not etym. related). The w of whole is post-OE; cf. Spenser's frequent spelling whot for hot (<hāt). Note the persistent long quantity of the whole group of words. The most persistent shared feature of etym. groups of words is the initial letter (if it is a consonant)--which is fortunate for philologists, because alphabetized lists of words provide the first clues of family relationships.
Cpd.: un-hǣlo.

21
    hām (m.) "dwelling, homestead, HOME."

Cognate with ModG Heim "home"; from a root meaning "to rest," probably cognate with Gk. keimai, koimāō, koitos "to lie, I put to sleep, bed," Lat. cūnae "cradle, nest."
Cpd.: hām-weorðung.

20
    blōd (n.) "BLOOD"; blōdiǧ (adj.) "bloody"; blōdeǧian (II) "make bloody."

Cognate with ModG Blut "blood."
Cpds.: blōd-fāg, -rēow; blōdiǧ-tōþ.

20
    brēost (n. or f.) "BREAST."

Cognate with ModG Brust "breast." It may be distantly related to OE byrne (No. 30), as "breast armor," but the words are not joined here. The sense of the etymon may be "swelling."
Cpds.: brēost-cearu, -cofa, -ǧehyǧd, -ǧewǣde, -hord, -nett, -weorðung, -wylm.

20
&#x1e21;ieldan (&#x1e21;eald, guldon, golden) (3) "YIELD, pay, give."

Most common as the cpd. for-&#x1e21;ieldan, with a sense of "re-
paying," sometimes of requiting or exacting vengeance.  Cognate with ModG gelten "to be valid" and with monetary terms
(YIELD, GUILD, ModG Geld "money").  The OE legal term wer-
geld is the "man-yield" (wer + &#x1e21;ield), the legal price of
a man, payable in cases of homicide.
Cpds.:  ā-, an-, for-&#x1e21;ieldan.


20
sār (n.) "pain, wound" (adj.) "SORE, grievous, painful";
sāre (adv.) "sorely"; sāri&#x1e21; (adj.) "sad."

The ModE noun SORE and the adj. SORRY (not related to OE
sorg > ModE sorrow) have both lost the idea of mortal pain
and grief of the OE words.  Cognate with ModG versehren
"to wound," the group may be related to Lat. saevus "raging."
Cpds.:  sār-līč; līč-sār; sāri&#x1e21;-ferþ, -mōd.


20
snot(t)or (adj.) "wise"; snyttru (wk.f.) "wisdom,
skill."

A fine word, remarkable in "The Wanderer," about which few
have cared to propose etym. speculation.
Cpds.:  snotor-līče; fore-snotor; un-snyttru.

Strong and Preterite-Present Verbs

This list includes all the strong and pret.-pres. verbs found in the Word-Hoard. The prefix ǧe- is here ignored. The first number, in parentheses, is the frequency of the individual verb together with all its forms with prefixes. The second number is the group frequency. The principal parts are explained in the Introduction.

## Strong Verbs

### Class 1

| (45) | 46 | bīdan | bād | bidon | biden | "BIDE" |
| (45) | 52 | wītan | wāt | witon | witen | "blame" |
| (1) | 37 | līðan | lāþ | lidon | liden | "go" |

### Class 2

| (21) | 63 | būgan | bēag | bugon | bogen | "BOW" |
| (16) | 117 | drēogan | drēag | drugon | drogen | "undergo" |
| (11) | 21 | flēon | flēah | flugon | flogen | "FLEE" |
| (9) | 23 | čēosan | čēas | curon | coren | "CHOOSE" |
| (5) | 23 | drēosan | drēas | druron | droren | "fall" |
| (3) | 36 | lēosan | lēas | luron | loren | "LOSE" |

### Class 3

| (82) | 102 | weorðan | wearþ | wurdon | worden | "become" |
| (36) | 78 | findan | fand | fundon | funden | "FIND" |
| (25) | 37 | friǧnan | fræǧn | frugnon | frugnen | "ask" |
| (18) | 38 | windan | wand | wundon | wunden | "WIND" |
| (16) | 30 | bindan | band | bundon | bunden | "BIND" |
| (10) | 38 | beorgan | bearg | burgon | borgen | "protect" |
| (7) | 150 | winnan | wann | wunnon | wunnen | "fight" |

### Class 4

| (74) | 90 | cuman | cōm | cōmon | cumen | "COME" |
| (50) | 140 | beran | bær | bēron | boren | "BEAR" |
| (44) | 44 | niman | nam | nāmon | numen | "take" |
| (1) | 82 | helan | hæl | hǣlon | holen | "conceal" |

### Class 5

| (57) | 78 | sēon | seah | sāwon | sewen | "SEE" |
| (45) | 64 | licgan | læǧ | lāgon | leǧen | "LIE" |
| (33) | 53 | wrecan | wræc | wrǣcon | wrecen | "avenge" |
| (32) | 67 | sittan | sæt | sǣton | seten | "SIT" |
| (29) | 81 | ǧiefan | ǧeaf | ǧēafon | ǧiefen | "GIVE" |
| (28) | 37 | cweðan | cwæþ | cwǣdon | cweden | "say" |

## Class 5 (continued)

| | | | | | |
|---|---|---|---|---|---|
| (27) | 28 | -ġietan | -ġeat | -ġēaton | -ġieten | "grasp" |
| (27) | 30 | sprecan | spræc | sprǣcon | sprecen | "SPEAK" |
| (17) | 21 | biddan | bæd | bǣdon | beden | "BID" |
| (12) | 49 | wegan | wæġ | wǣgon | weġen | "carry" |
| (4) | 37 | fricgan | | | frǣġen | "ask" |
| (4) | 39 | metan | mæt | mǣton | meten | "measure" |
| (1) | 93 | wegan | wæġ | wǣgon | weġen | "fight" |

## Class 6

| | | | | | |
|---|---|---|---|---|---|
| (62) | 128 | standan | stōd | stōdon | standen | "STAND" |
| (23) | 26 | slēan | slōg | slōgon | slæġen | "strike" |
| (14) | 69 | faran | fōr | fōron | faren | "GO" |
| (11) | 32 | scieþþan | scōd | scōdon | sceaðen | "harm" |
| (5) | 50 | scieppan | scōp | scōpon | scapen | "create" |
| (2) | 81 | sacan | sōc | sōcon | sacen | "fight" |

## Class 7

| | | | | | |
|---|---|---|---|---|---|
| (77) | 80 | healdan | hēold | hēoldon | healden | "HOLD" |
| (36) | 101 | gangan | ġēong | ġēongon | gangen | "go" |
| (33) | 37 | lǣtan | lēt | lēton | lǣten | "LET" |
| (25) | 33 | fōn | fēng | fēngon | fangen | "seize" |
| (24) | 62 | wealdan | wēold | wēoldon | wealden | "rule" |
| (23) | 37 | feallan | fēoll | fēollon | feallen | "FALL" |
| (17) | 37 | weallan | wēoll | wēollon | weallen | "surge" |
| (8) | 57 | hātan | hēt | hēton | hāten | "call" |
| (6) | 28 | weaxan | wēox | wēoxon | weaxen | "grow" |
| (4) | 23 | rǣdan | rēd | rēdon | rǣden | "counsel" |
| (1) | 90 | cnāwan | cnēow | cnēowon | cnāwen | "KNOW" |
| (1) | 22 | flōwan | flēow | flēowon | flōwen | "FLOW" |

### Preterite-Present Verbs

| | | | | | |
|---|---|---|---|---|---|
| (119) | 124 | sculan | sceal | scealt | sceolde | "ought to" |
| (116) | 170 | magan | mæġ | meaht | meahte | "be able" |
| (46) | 46 | *mōtan | mōt | mōst | mōste | "may" |
| (34) | 96 | witan (nytan) | wāt | wāst | wiste | "know" |
| (30) | 61 | ġemunan | ġeman | ġemanst | ġemunde | "be mindful of" |
| (25) | 90 | cunnan | cann | canst | cūðe | "know (how), can" |
| (19) | 43 | *þurfan | þearf | þearft | þorfte | "need" |
| (18) | 33 | āgan (nāgan) | āh | āhst | āhte | "possess" |
| (10) | 41 | dugan | dēag | | dohte | "be good for" |

# Words Easy to Confuse

Like any lang., OE has many words which are homophones or near-homophones of others, and liable to be confused. The variety of spellings of many words only increases the liability. From this Word-Hoard the following words may trouble you:

1. bǣl (n.) "fire" and bealu (n.) "malice, pain, BALE."

2. ǧebeorg (n.) "defense" and beorg (m.) "hill."

3. beorn (m.) "warrior, man" and bearn (n.) "child, son."

4. bīdan (1) "await, BIDE, remain" and ǧe-bīdan (1) "live to experience" and biddan (5) "BID, urge, pray" and bǣdan (I) "compel, urge, constrain" and bēodan (2) "offer, announce, foreBODE."

5. cennan (I) "declare, show, make known" and cennan (I) "beget."

6. cunnan (pret.-pres.) "know (how)" and cunnian (II) "test, try, experience."

7. ealdor (or aldor) (m.) "chief, lord" and ealdor (aldor) (n.) "life."

8. fær (n.) "ship" and fǣr (m.) "sudden attack."

9. fāh/fāg (adj.) "hostile, outlawed" and fāg/fāh (adj.) "decorated, variegated, shining, stained."

10. fēran (I) "go, journey" and ǧe-fēran (I) "reach" and faran (6) "go, FARE" and ǧe-faran (6) "proceed, act" and ferian (I) "carry, lead, bring."

11. flēon (2) "FLEE" and flēogan (2) "FLY" (confused in OE).

12. frēa (wk.m.) "lord" and frēo (adj.) "free, noble" and frēo (f.) "lady."

13. gāst/gǣst (m.) "soul, spirit, GHOST" and ǧiest/ǧist/gæst (m.) "stranger, GUEST."

14. hēah (adj.) (wk. forms: hēan; acc. sg. m. hēanne) "HIGH" and hēan (adj.) "lowly, abject, despised."

15. herian (I) "praise" and herian (II) "plunder, assail, HARRY."

16. lēod (m.) "man" and lēode (pl.) "people" and lēod (f.) "people, nation."

17. mǣǧ (m.) (pl. mǣgas) "kinsman" and magu/mago (m.) "son, young man" and maga (wk.m.) "son, young man."

18. mǣl (n.) (in cpds.) "measure" or "mark, sign" and mǣl (n.) "speech" and mǣl (n.) "time, occasion."

19. man(n) (m.) "man" and mān (n.) "crime, guilt."

20. oþþe/oþþæt (conj.) "until" and oþþe (conj.) "OR" and oþ (prep.) "up to."

21. sīþ (m.) "journey, exploit" and sīþ (comp. adv.) "later."

22. stefn (m.) "stem, prow, stern of a ship, or trunk of a tree" and stefna (wk.m.) "stem of a ship" and stefn (m.) "period, time" and stefn (f.) "voice" (ModG stimme).

23. symbel (n.) (dat. sg. symle) "feast" and symle/symble/simble (adv.) "always."

24. syn-/sin- "ever, perpetual, great" and syn- "sinful."

25. þenčan (I) "think, intend" and þynčan (I) "seem, appear."

26. wegan (5) "carry" and ģe-wegan (5) "fight" and wīgan (I) "fight."

27. weorðan (3) "become, happen, be" and weorðian (II) "honor, adorn."

28. windan (3) "WIND, wave, twist" wunden (ppl. adj.) "twisted" and wund (f.) "WOUND, injury" and wund (adj.) "WOUNDed."

29. wine (m.) "friend, friendly lord" and wīn (n.) "WINE" (the beverage).

30. wītan (1) "blame, impute" and ģe-wītan (1) "go, depart" and witan (pret.-pres.) "know."

31. wrecan (5) (pret. 3 sg. wræc) "drive, force, utter, avenge" and ģe-wrecan (5) "avenge" and wracu (f.) (acc. sg. wræce) "misery, revenge" and wræc (n.) "misery, persecution, exile" and reččan (I) "narrate" and rečan/reččan (I) "care about" and rēčan (I) "REACH."

## False Friends

The "Index to the Groups" shows several examples of ModE reflexes of OE words which no longer have the same meaning, and which frequently confuse the beginning student. Here is a list of some which appear in this Word-Hoard. (Note that the pret.-pres. verbs are special offenders.)

| | | | |
|---|---|---|---|
| cræftiġ normally means not | "crafty" | BUT | "powerful" |
| cunnan | "can" | | "know (how)" |
| dōm | "doom" | | "judgement" |
| drēam | "dream" | | "festivity" |
| drēoriġ | "dreary" | | "bloody" or "grieving" |
| eorl | "earl" | | "warrior", "nobleman" |
| folc | "folk" | | "army" |
| grimm | "grim" | | "fierce" |
| magan | "may" | | "can, be able" |
| mōd | "mood" | | "mind, spirit" |
| *mōtan | "must" | | "may, be permitted" |
| rīċe | "rich" | | "powerful" |
| sār | "sore" | | "grievous" |
| scēawian | "show" | | "look at, examine" |
| sculan | "shall" | | "ought to" |
| sellan | "sell" | | "give" |
| slēan | "slay" | | "strike" |
| þynċan | "think" | | "seem" |
| willan | "will" | | "wish" |
| winnan | "win" | | "contend" |
| wiþ | "with" | | "against" |

This list aims to include all the words cited in Word-Hoard.
It is not intended to serve as a glossary. For quick reference,
turn to the "Index to the Groups" which follows this Index at the
end of the book. Teachers may find this full index useful: an
examination can be set or a text assigned which glosses only
words not found in this index. Note that only words drawn from
the headlists are normalized: you may have to look under y (less
often i) for a "normal" ie (ġyfu/ġiefu), under o for an a (mon/
mann), under h for a g (burh/burg), under o for a u (beado-/beadu-).
The ge- prefix is not regarded in the alphabetizing. The character æ is alphabetized after ad; þ and ð are alphabetized together
as if they were the same letter, after t. The number in parentheses after a word is the individual frequency of that word in our
texts. A second number, not in parentheses, is the frequency of
the group in which the word occurs, and so refers to the group-
frequency numbers in the main list of the Word-Hoard. Compound
words may show three numbers: the count of the occurrences of the
compound alone (in parentheses), then the group frequencies of
each base. So [weorodrǣdend (1) 23, 23] is a word that occurs
once in our texts, and it is listed under both weorod (No. 23)
and rǣd (by chance, also No. 23). Words followed by only one number (e.g., ǣr-) do not occur as separate words in our texts in
one of their senses--here in the sense "early"--but were included
in the headlists of the groups as bases of compounds which do occur.

| | | |
|---|---|---|
| ā, āwa (12) 97 | ǣġhwylċ (13) 201 | ǣrra (3) 114 |
| ābīdan (1) 46 | ǣġðer (2) 201 | ǣrþon (1) 114 |
| ābūgan (1) 64 | ǣġweard (1) 55 | ǣrwela (1) 114, 162 |
| ac (72) 72 | ǣht (4) 33 | æschere (1) 28 |
| ācennan (1) 116 | ǣledlēoma (1) 39 | æscwiga (1) 93 |
| ācweðan (3) 37 | ælmihtiġ (9)159, 170 | æt (85) 85 |
| ācȳðan (1) 90 | ælwiht (1) 25 | ætberan (7) 140 |
| ādrēogan (1) 117 | ǣne (1) 124 | ætferian (1) 69 |
| æfengrom (1) 36 | (n)ǣniġ (51) 124 | ætforan (1) 141 |
| æfenlēoht (1) 39 | ǣnlīċ (3) 124 | ætgædere (9) 31 |
| æfensprǣc (1) 30 | ǣr (85) 114 | ætġiefan (1) 81 |
| æfre (10) 97 | ǣr- 114 | æthweorfan (1) 27 |
| æftan (1) 197 | ǣrdæġ (3) 59, 114 | ætrihte (1) 23 |
| æfter (77) 197 | ǣrest (12) 114 | ætstandan (1) 128 |
| æftercweðende (1) 37, | ǣrfæder (1) 24, 114 | ætwegan (1) 49 |
| 197 | ǣrġestrēon (2) 114 | ætwindan (1) 38 |
| æfþunca (1) 72 | ǣrġeweorc (1) 114 | ætwītan (3) 52 |
| ǣġ- 97 | ǣrġewinn (1) 114, 150 | (ġe-)æðele (8) 65 |
| ǣġhwā (5) 201 | ǣrġōd (5) 114, 129 | æðeling (33) 65 |
| ǣġhwǣr (1) 201 | ǣror (4) 114 | æðelu (5) 65 |

KEY-WORD INDEX TO THE GROUPS

The words listed here are the head-words and a selection of other important words from the Word-Hoard. The numbers are the frequency numbers of the groups to which the words belong. Words printed in capital letters are the ModE reflexes of the etymological group, but not necessarily of the particular form here. Items lacking words in capitals have no obvious ModE reflex.

ac "but" 72
ǣfre "EVER" 97
æfter "AFTER" 197
ǣniġ "ANY" 124
ǣr "before" (ERE) 114
æt "AT" 85
æðele "noble" 65
āgan "OWN" 33
āglǣca "monster" 22
ān "ONE" 124
bana "slayer" (BANE) 27
be "BY" 79
bēag "ring" (BOW) 64
bealu "BALE" 29
beorg "hill" (iceBERG) 21
beorgan "protect" (BURG) 38
beorht "BRIGHT" 22
beorn "warrior" 36
beran "BEAR" 140
bīdan "BIDE" 46
biddan "BID" 21
bindan "BIND" 30
blōd "BLOOD" 20
bord "shield" (BOARD) 24
brēost "BREAST" 20
būgan "BOW" 64
burg "stronghold" (BURG) 38
byrne "corselet" (BYRNIE) 30
ċēosan "CHOOSE" 23
cræft "strength" (CRAFT) 24
cuman "COME" 90
cunnan "know" (CAN) 90
cūþ "KNOWN" 90
cweðan "say" (beQUEATH) 37
cyning "KING" 116
cynn "family" (KINdred) 116
cȳþþ "home" (KITH) 90

dæġ "DAY" 59
dǣl "share" (DEAL) 30
dēaþ "DEATH" 40
dōm "judgement" (DOOM) 99
dōn "DO" 99
drēam "festivity" (DREAM) 22
drēogan "undergo" (DREE) 117
drēoriġ "bloody" (DREARY) 23
drēosan "fall" (DREARY) 23
dryhten "lord" (DREE) 117
dugan "be good (for)" (DOUGHTY) 41
ēac "also" (EKE) 28
eald "OLD" 131
ealdor "life/chief" (OLD) 131
eall "ALL" 159
eard "homeland" 22
ēċe "eternal" (EVER) 97
ecg "EDGE, sword" 42
ellen "valor" 43
ende "END" 23
eorl "nobleman" (EARL) 77
eorðe "EARTH" 53
fæder "FATHER" 24
fæst "firm" (FAST) 56
fāg "variegated" 36
fāh "hostile" (FEUD) 35
faran "go" (FARE) 69
feallan "FALL" 37
fela "much" (FULL) 97
fēond "enemy" (FIEND) 34
feorh "life" 88
feorr "FAR" 41
fēða "infantry" (FIND) 78
findan "FIND" 78
flēon "FLEE" 21
flōd "FLOOD" 22

105